PRIMER ON EFFECT SIZES, SIMPLE RESEARCH DESIGNS, AND CONFIDENCE INTERVALS

PRIMER ON EFFECT SIZES, SIMPLE RESEARCH DESIGNS, AND CONFIDENCE INTERVALS

By

MARTY SAPP

Professor
Department of Educational Psychology
University of Wisconsin-Milwaukee

CHARLES C THOMAS • PUBLISHER, LTD.
Springfield • Illinois • U.S.A.

Published and Distributed Throughout the World by

CHARLES C THOMAS • PUBLISHER, LTD.
2600 South First Street
Springfield, Illinois 62704

This book is protected by copyright. No part of
it may be reproduced in any manner without written
permission from the publisher. All rights reserved.

© 2017 by CHARLES C THOMAS • PUBLISHER, LTD.

ISBN 978-0-398-09197-2 (paper)
ISBN 978-0-398-09198-9 (ebook)

With THOMAS BOOKS *careful attention is given to all details of manufacturing and design. It is the Publisher's desire to present books that are satisfactory as to their physical qualities and artistic possibilities and appropriate for their particular use.* THOMAS BOOKS *will be true to those laws of quality that assure a good name and good will.*

Printed in the United States of America

TO-C-1

Library of Congress Cataloging-in-Publication Data

Names: Sapp, Marty, 1958- author.
Title: Primer on effect sizes, simple research designs, and confidence
    intervals / by Marty Sapp, Professor, Department of Educational
    Psychology, University of Wisconsin-Milwaukee.
Description: Springfield, Illinois : Charles C Thomas, Publisher, [2017] |
    Includes bibliographical references and index.
Identifiers: LCCN 2017031574 (print) | LCCN 2017046235 (ebook) |
    ISBN 9780398091989 (ebook) | ISBN 9780398091972 (pbk)
Subjects: LCSH: Psychometrics. | Psychology--Statistical methods. |
    Psychology--Methodology.
Classification: LCC BF39 (ebook) | LCC BF39 .S2653 2017 (print) | DDC
    150.72/1--dc23
LC record available at https://lccn.loc.gov/2017031574

PREFACE

A Primer on Effect Sizes, Simple Research Designs, and Confidence Intervals was designed to help individuals learn to calculate effect sizes for their research designs. Effect sizes allow a clinician or researcher to determine the effect of a treatment. For example, an effect size of zero would indicate that the treatment had no effect, but generally, effect sizes allow researchers to see the degree of effect of some treatment or intervention. Often, researchers and clinicians are not aware that effect sizes are connected to research designs. For years, statisticians have been aware of limits of null hypothesis significance testing (NHST). The Wilkinson Task Force (Wilkinson & Task Force on Statistical Inference, 1999) recommended that researchers report effect sizes and confidence intervals in addition to null hypothesis significance testing (NHST).

A sample effect size allows a researcher or clinician to determine the effect size for his or her sample data, but a confidence interval around an effect size allows one to describe the effect size within a given population. Since 1999, the reporting of effect sizes by researchers has been inconsistent. Also, some researchers and some statisticians have little guidance and understanding of effect sizes. Realistically speaking, there are many effect size measures and researchers need some guidelines on how to calculate these simple statistics and how to interpret them. Recently, in 2015, the journal *Basic and Applied Social Psychology* banned null hypothesis significance testing (NHST). The Publication Manual of the American Psychological Association encourages the reporting of effect sizes with inferential test statistics. Also, this manual encourages the reporting of confidence intervals. The purpose of this book is to provide the connection among effect sizes, confidence intervals, and simple research designs. Also, some commonly used univariate and multivariate statistics are covered. Regression discontinuity designs, simple moderation and mediation designs, power analysis, and fit indices as effect sizes measure are presented. All calculations are demonstrated through a calculator and statistical packages such as Microsoft Excel, SPSS, SAS, and Hayes' Process Analysis. This book covers more than 25 effect sizes that are connected to simple research designs.

This book will be of interest to students taking a statistics class, research methods class, or research design class. Unlike many texts within this area, the current text will give students or researchers the understanding of how to calculate effect sizes with a simple calculator or with a few commands from statistical software programs. Hence, mathematical ability is not a prerequisite for this text. This text provides a nonmathematical treatment of effect sizes within the context of research designs. Finally, to aid understanding, critical material is repeated throughout this book.

CONTENTS

	Page
Preface	v

Chapter
1. INTRODUCTION: R AND D EFFECT SIZES 3
   History of Effect Sizes 3
   Reliability for Unidimensional Scales 8
   Reliability for Multidimensional Scales.................... 13
   Validity... 13
   Face Validity....................................... 14
   Content Validity 15
   Criterion Validity 15
   Predictive Validity 16
   Construct Validity................................. 18
   Effect Sizes 23
   Definition of Multivariate Statistics 25
   Confidence Intervals 27
   Testing Calculated Validity Coefficients Against
      Hypothesized Values 28
   Standard Error of Estimate 30
   Confidence Intervals Around Validity..................... 30
   A Practical Example of a One Sample Case 95%
      Confidence Interval 32
   Discussion... 34
   The Effect Size r.................................. 36
   Counternull Value of an Effect......................... 39
   Meta-Analysis...................................... 39
   Confidence Intervals Around the Effect Size r 47
   Using SAS for Calculating d Effect Size Confidence Intervals... 53

SAS Control Lines to Compute an Exact 95% Confidence
   Interval for Effect Size d For Two Groups of Participants... 54
SAS Control Lines to Compute an Exact 95% Confidence
   Interval for Effect Size d For One Group of Participants ... 55
Chapter Summary 56
Practice Problems... 57
Answer to Practice Problems 58

2. CONFIDENCE INTERVALS FOR A SINGLE MEAN 59
   Problems.. 61
   Answers... 62

3. EFFECT SIZE AND CONFIDENCE INTERVAL
   FOR DIFFERENCES BETWEEN TWO MEANS
   (Between Group Research Designs) 63
       Regression Discontinuity Designs 66

4. ONE-GROUP PRE-TEST POST-TEST DESIGN............. 68
   Problems.. 70
   Answers... 70

5. EFFECT SIZE FOR ONE-WAY ANALYSIS OF VARIANCE
   OR THREE OR MORE GROUP MEANS................... 72
       Test of Between-Subjects Effects 76
       Test of Homogeneity of Variances......................... 76
       SAS Commands for 95% Confidence Interval for Eta Squared.. 77
       Welch and Brown-Forsythe Test for Unequal Variances........ 77
       Factorial Designs 80
       Fixed Effects, Random Effects, and Mixed Model Analysis of
          Variance (ANOVA) 84
       Disproportional Cell Size or Unbalanced Factorial Designs 86
       Three-Way Analysis of Variance (ANOVA) 89
       Multiple Comparisons 90
       Post Hoc Procedures...................................... 95
       Nested ANOVA 96
       One-Way Analysis of Covariance (ANCOVA)............... 101

6. CORRELATIONS AS EFFECT SIZES 108

7. EFFECT SIZES FOR TWO OR MORE PREDICTORS
   AND ONE DEPENDENT VARIABLE.................... 122
   Multiple Regression 122
   Schematic Design for Two-Predictor Case........ 123
   Analysis of Variance Table for Regression 125
   Multiple Regression Broken Down into Sums of Squares 126
   Assumptions of Multiple Regression............. 126
   Suppressor Variables in Multiple Regression ... 127
   Structure Coefficients within Multiple Regression 130
   Interaction Effects within Multiple Regression............ 130
   Cross-Validation Formulas with Multiple Regression........ 131
   Logistic Regression............................ 135

8. EFFECT SIZES FOR TWO OR MORE PREDICTORS
   AND TWO OR MORE DEPENDENT VARIABLES 139
   Multivariate Regression 139

9. EFFECT SIZE FOR TWO-GROUP MULTIVARIATE
   ANALYSIS OF VARIANCE 143
   Discussion..................................... 147

10. MODERATION AND MEDITATION EFFECTS 148

11. POWER ANALYSIS................................ 156
    A Priori and Post Hoc Estimations of Power.... 157

12. PATH ANALYSIS AND EFFECT SIZES.............. 160

13. FIT INDICES AS EFFECT SIZE MEASURES 163
    Book Summary.................................. 164

References 169
Name Index.. 175
Subject Index..................................... 177

PRIMER ON EFFECT SIZES, SIMPLE RESEARCH DESIGNS, AND CONFIDENCE INTERVALS

Chapter 1

INTRODUCTION: R AND D EFFECT SIZES

HISTORY OF EFFECT SIZES

Huberty (2002) found that the history of effect size started around 1940. The correlation ratio or eta coefficient was proposed during the 1940s. The correlation ratio is used to measure curvilinear relationships. In addition, eta measures the relationship between a grouping variable and a dependent or outcome variable. During this period, eta squared was connected to ANOVA to show the variance accounted for on a dependent variable. Suppose 20 participants were randomly assigned to four groups, and let us assume the groups and data are the following:

Group	*Dependent Variable*
1	53
1	54
1	52
1	55
1	54
2	53
2	56
2	57
2	55
3	57
3	56
3	54
3	58
3	59
3	58
4	62

4	62
4	61
4	60
4	56

The groups 1 through 4 is the grouping variable. In other words, a grouping variable is the levels of an independent variable. Eta squared equals between sum of squares divided by the total sum of squares. Eta Squared=118.050/172.800=.683.

Eta=.826. Cohen characterized eta squared of .01 as a small effect size, an eta squared of .06 as a medium effect size, and an eta squared of .14 as a large effect size.

The .683 is the variance accounted for on the dependent variable, and .826 is the correlation of the group identifications with the dependent variable. Ronald A. Fisher (1890–1961), in 1924, derived the probability of eta in the context of ANOVA. Truman (1935) Kelley (1884–1961) proposed an adjustment to the eta squared within the context of ANOVA. Some statisticians refer to this as the partial eta squared. The psychologist William L. Hays (1926–1995) in his popular textbook, proposed omega squared as an alternative to eta squared (Hays, 1981). Omega squared is said to be derived through unbiased estimates. Omega squared =SSB-(K-1)MSW/(SST+MSW). Where SSB equals the sum of squares between and K equals the number of groups. MSW is the mean squares within, and SST is the total sum of squares. Generally, omega squared and eta squared will not differ much. If the levels of the grouping variable (independent variable) are random, in contrast to being fixed, the intraclass correlation coefficient can be used as an effect size. The formula for the intraclass correlation R is the following:

$$R=(MSB-MSW)/[MSB+(n-1)MSW]$$

MSB and MSW are the numerator and denominator from an F statistic or test and n equals the number of participants per group.

In summary, at least three strengths of relationship effect sizes were proposed between 1935 to 1963: eta squared, omega squared, and the intraclass correlation coefficient. Karl Pearson (1857–1936), in 1910, proposed the biserial correlation coefficient. It is used when a continuous variable is forced into a discrete variable and is correlated with a continuous variable. For example, suppose we were interested in the correlation between hypnotizablity and creative imagination. Both of these variables are continuous, but we forced the hypnotizability scores into high and low hypnotizability. The correlation between these two variables would be the biserial correlation coefficient. The biserial correlation coefficient cannot be used in regression in order to predict y values or dependent variables. Also, confidence intervals cannot be placed around the biserial correlation coefficient. Finally, the biserial correlation coefficient is less reliable than the Pearson correlation coefficient, and it is not recommended as an effect size (Sapp, 2015).

Jacob Cohen, in 1969, proposed an effect size for a two group mean comparison, and Huberty (2002) referred to these as group differences indices. Cohen defined his effect size as the differences between means divided by the pool standard deviation across the two groups. Like Cohen, the statistician Gene V. Glass also proposed a d effect size as the differences between means divided by the control group standard deviation. In addition, the statistician Larry V. Hedges (1982) took exception with Cohen and Glass, and he proposed an adjusted d that he called g (Huberty, 2002). Cohen also proposed a standard difference type of effect size for multiple groups or multiple means context (ANOVA), and he used the letter f as this effect size, and it is the following formula:

$$f=[(K-1)F/N]^{1/2}$$

K is the number of groups, and F is the F statistics from ANOVA. N is the total group size. When using Cohen's power tables, the average group size is used or the harmonic mean if the group sizes are unequal. The f effect size can be seen as the standard deviation of the standardized means, or the variability of the group means relative to the standard deviation (Huberty, 2002). Cohen (1977) characterized f equals .10 as a small effect size, f=.25 as a medium effect size, and f>.40 as a large effect size.

Huberty (2002) discussed another effect size based on overlap indices. Within a two-group situation, if two have a large amount of overlap the effect size will be small. Cohen (1977) also defined d as the percent of non-overlap of the treatment group scores with those of the untreated group. For example, the following shows various effect sizes and percent of non-overlap.

Cohen's standard	d Effect Size	Percent of Non-overlap
	4.0	97.7
	3.8	97.0
	3.6	96.3
	3.4	95.3
	3.2	94.2
	3.0	92.8
	2.8	91.2
	2.6	89.3
	2.4	87.0
	2.2	84.3
	2.0	81.1
	1.9	79.4
	1.8	77.4
	1.7	75.4
	1.6	73.1
	1.5	70.7
	1.4	68.1
	1.3	65.3
	1.2	62.2
	1.1	58.9
	1.0	55.4
	.9	51.6
Large	**.8**	**47.4**
	.7	43.0
	.6	38.2
Medium	**.5**	**33.0**
	.4	27.4
	.3	21.3
Small	**.2**	**14.7**
	.1	7.7
	0	
	1	

An effect size of zero indicates that the distribution of scores of the treatment group overlap completely with the distribution of the control group. Cohen (1977) provided the following rough guidelines for interpreting the d effect size:

d = .2 small effect size, d = .5 medium effect size, and d = .8 large effect size.

One should not just blindly accept these standards based on Cohen's work but interpret effect sizes within a given professional area.

The r effect size and d effect size are related in that $r = \frac{d}{\sqrt{d^2+4}}$. Also, d can be expressed as t using the following formula: $d = t(1/n1 = 1/n2)^{1/2}$. The t is the value from a t test, and the n1 and n2 are the respective group sizes.

The following is the relationship between r and d:

	d effect size	r effect size
	4.0	.894
	3.8	.885
	3.6	.874
	3.4	.862
	3.2	.848
	3.0	.832
	2.8	.814
	2.6	.793
	2.4	.768
	2.2	.740
	2.0	.707
	1.9	.689
	1.8	.669
	1.7	.648
	1.6	.625
	1.5	.600
	1.4	.573
	1.3	.545
	1.2	.514
	1.1	.482
	1.0	.447
	.9	.410
large	**.8**	**.371**
	.7	.330
	.6	.287
medium	**.5**	**.243**
	.4	.196
	.3	.148
small	**.2**	**.100**
	.1	.050
	0	0

With his history of effect sizes, the final group of effect sizes that Huberty discussed were the multivariate indices (Huberty, 2002). The concept of multiple regression or the multiple correlation coefficient was developed in 1914 by Pearson and Lee (1897). Cohen's f^2 equals $R^2/(1-R^2)$. R is the multiple correlation coefficient. Multivariate Analysis of Variance (MANOVA) is applicable to a two or more group variable situation where participants are measured on two or more dependent or outcome variables. Maurice M. Tatsuoka (1922–1996) summarized the literature in this area in 1973. Tatsuoka (1970) connected Samuel S. Wilks' (1906–1964) Lambda to the MANOVA context as a measure of multivariate strength of association. The smaller the value of Wilks' Lambda, the stronger the multivariate effect.

After reviewing several journals within the counseling and psychological literature, I found few studies addressing basic measurement issues, effect sizes, and confidence intervals. With this is in mind, the purpose of this section is to address these factors. Because sufficient narrative is used in place of formulas, I hope that researchers can apply these concepts to their research.

RELIABILITY FOR UNIDIMENSIONAL SCALES

In theory, there are reliabilities for unidimensional scales and for multidimensional scales. Often researchers will use a unidimensional reliability on a multidimensional scale. Classical test theory is the model often taught in introductory psychological measurement courses for finding reliability. Psychologists have used this theory of measurement since the turn of the 20th century. Many times, it is used to find reliability measures such as test-retest, internal consistency, and so on. It is also referred to as the true score, and it has the following mathematical model:

$$X = T + E$$
X = a person's score or an observed score
T = a person's true score
E = the error score

Theoretically, reliability can be expressed as the ratio of true score variance divided by the observed score variance. If we symbolize reliability as r_{xx}, it can be expressed mathematically as:

$$r_{xx} = \frac{S_t^2}{S_x^2} = \frac{\text{true score variance}}{\text{observed score variance}}$$

A specific form of reliability, called coefficient alpha, is defined by two quantities. First, the number of test items divided by the number of test items minus one. The second quantity is one minus the sum of item variances divided by the total test variance. Finally, these quantities are multiplied. In summary, coefficient alpha, like other forms of reliability fits the definition involving variances. The following is the formula for coefficient alpha:

$$K/(K-1)\left[1 - \frac{\Sigma S_i^2}{S_t^2}\right]$$

where K equals the number of items
ΣS_i^2 equals the variance for across test items
ΣS_t^2 equals the variance for the participants' total test scores.

Verbally, coefficient alpha is the following:

$$\frac{\text{No. of Items}}{\text{No. of Items} - 1}\left[1 - \frac{\text{Sum of Item Variances}}{\text{Test Variance}}\right]$$

Sapp (2015) recommended interpreting test scores using the standard error of measurement. This index measures the amount of error within test items. Essentially, this is the standard deviation for a set of items, and this formula is the following:

$$S_e = S_x \sqrt{1 - r_{xx}}$$

Reliability is the variance that is accounted for on a set of test items; hence, it is a squared correlation or squared area. With the area of hypnosis, reliability is the percent of variance accounted for on a hypnosis measure. Once a hypnosis test is standardized, the reliability that is reported in a manual is the reliability measure for the standardization sample, but this value does not tell one how another independent sample will respond to those test items; therefore, within the twenty-first century, measurement theorists make a distinction between reliability of the standardization sample and reliability of an independent sample. The important point is that reliability involves how individuals respond to test items; hence, reliability is not invariant; meaning it does not change from sample to sample. The only way to know reliability for a given sample is to calculate it. In essence, reliability is the consistency that a sample responds to a set of test items. Sadly, within a multicultural perspective, often minorities are not included within the standardization process for available hypnosis tests.

There are four commonly reported forms of reliability: test-retest, alternative forms, internal consistence, and inter-rater or inter-scorer. Test-retest reliability is the administration of the same test under two conditions to the same set of individuals, and these two sets of scores are correlated to produce a reliability coefficient.

Suppose 5 minority college students were pre-tested and post-test on the Stanford Hypnotic Susceptibility Scale, Form C, and the following are their artificial test scores.

Participants	Pre-test	Post-test
1	2	3
2	1	2
3	6	5
4	9	8
5	8	7

This example is used to show how to calculate test-retest reliability using the SPPS computer software. The following are the SPSS codes for running this analysis:

```
CORRELATIONS
 /VARIABLES=pretest posttest
 /PRINT=TWOTAIL NOSIG
 /MISSING=PAIRWISE.
```

The following was the output from this analysis:

Correlations

		Pre-test	Post-test
pretest	Pearson Correlation	1	.991(*)
	Sig. (2-tailed)		.001
	N	5	5
posttest	Pearson Correlation	.991(*)	1
	Sig. (2-tailed)	.001	
	N	5	5

Correlation is significant at the 0.01 level (2-tailed).

From the output, the Pearson correlation .991, and the numeral five indicates that we have five pairs of scores. The .991 indicates that 99.1% of the variability on the post-test is the result of true-score variability and 100% minus 99.1% equals .9% of the variability is error. This is the application of the true score formula. Again, as previously stated, reliability is a squared correlation because of the true score theory. This test-retest reliability represents the consistency of participants' scores over time. Readers may remember that reliability values range from zero to a positive one. Between set of scores, the higher the reliability value, the stronger the relationship.

Alternative forms reliability is the construction of two equivalent forms of the same hypnosis test and administering both forms to the same groups of individuals, and the correlation of the items from the two equivalent tests represent a reliability of equivalence.

Inter-scorer or inter-rater reliability is often necessary when scoring of test items deal with subjective or ambiguous stimuli. For example, creativity or projective tests of personality can be scored by using raters. This form of reliability is found by having two or more people rate test items, and then these ratings are correlated.

Internal consistency can determine the consistency of test items. Coefficient alpha is the most used measure of internal consistency. Suppose that 12 Latino American college students completed 6 items that measured dissociation, and these items were rated on a 4-point scale. The following output from SPSS has coefficient alpha, and the 95% confidence interval around the population coefficient alpha. These data for this example are the following:

These data that follow are in the following form: participant, item 1, item 2, item 3, item 4, item5, and item 6:

1.	1	2	3	1	4	1
2.	1	1	1	1	1	1
3.	1	1	2	2	4	2
4.	3	3	3	3	3	3
5.	1	2	3	4	4	2
6.	1	2	3	4	4	1
7.	2	1	3	3	3	4
8.	2	1	4	4	4	1
9.	2	1	3	4	3	2
10.	2	2	4	3	3	3
11.	2	2	3	3	3	3
12.	2	2	4	3	3	4

The SPSS control lines for these data are the following:

```
RELIABILITY
  /VARIABLES=item1 item2 item3 item4 item5 item6
  /SCALE('ALL VARIABLES')  ALL/MODEL=ALPHA
  /STATISTICS=DESCRIPTIVE SCALE CORR ANOVA
  /ICC=MODEL(MIXED) TYPE(CONSISTENCY) CIN=95
  TESTVAL=0.
```

The following are the output for coefficient alpha:

Reliability Statistics

Cronbach's Alpha	Cronbach's Alpha Based on Standardized Items	N of Items
.691	.709	6

Coefficient alpha or Cronbach's alpha was .691. This tell us that 69.1% on these items is true score variance, and 1-.691, and .309 or 30.9 % is the error variance. Is summary, the point estimate, or alpha for this sample data was .691. Later, when confidence intervals are discussed, a confidence interval will be provided for the population coefficient alpha. Finally, coefficient alpha was designed for unidimensional scales.

RELIABILITY FOR MULTIDIMENSIONAL SCALES

When unidimensional reliabilities are applied to multidimensional scales, these reliabilities tend to be lower than ones applied to unidimensional scales. Principal components analysis and factor analysis are two common methods for determining the dimensionality of a scale. For multidimensional scales that have submitted to a principal components analysis, reliability can be estimated from the first principal component before rotation. Theta is the multidimensional reliability coefficient of coefficient alpha. Rosenthal and Rosnow (1984) provided the following formula for coefficient theta:

$$Theta = N/(N-1)(L-1/L)$$

N is the number of scale items or variables, and L is the eigenvalue, sum of the squared loading, before rotation. A loading is the correlation between a variable and component or factor. Unless a scale is unidimensional, one should not apply coefficient alpha. If several subscales make up a larger scale, coefficient alpha can be applied to each subscale and theta can be calculated for the entire scale. If one performs a factor analysis, the coefficient omega is the appropriate multidimensional reliability measure. Readers can consult Helms, Henze and Sass (2006) for a thorough discussion of omega. If one uses a unidimensional reliability on scale that is theoretically multidimensional, it makes sense to support the unidimensional reliability with a multidimensional one. In practice, I have found the results from both forms of reliability were very similar.

VALIDITY

Validity determines if items measure what they are meant to measure. Like reliability, since minorities are seldom included within standardization samples, validity indices are often questionable when applied to minorities. Often, when researchers speak about validity, they are referring to criterion validity. Criterion validity tells the degree that items from two tests correlate. Sapp (2006) reported that validity coefficients tend to fall with .20 and .60. Unlike reliability coefficients, validity coefficients must be squared to find the variance account for, or the coefficient of determination. For example, a validity coefficient of .5 states that .25 or 25% of the variance can be explained, and 75% of the variance is unexplained.

Even though the definition of **validity** is simple–test items measure what they purport to measure; however, clinicians and researchers often disagree on definitions of validity. This is because validity is a complex area involving several types of validity such as face, content, criterion, predictive, concurrent, and so on.

Within a psychological or educational instrument, test items may appear to have validity for one clinician or researcher, but another clinician or researcher may strongly contest that the items obtained from the instrument in question lack validity. Often, clinicians and researchers establish validity by correlating the items from participants taken from two tests or instruments. This measure is referred to as a **validity coefficient**; however, as the reader will see, things are seldom this simple. The following section will describe the simplest form of validity, face validity.

FACE VALIDITY

Because there are a variety of validities, readers often confuse research-related validities–internal validity and external validity–with test scores-related validities (Sapp, 2006). Sapp (2006) defined **internal validity** as an experimental process in which a researcher can logically conclude that some treatment or independent variable produced changes on a dependent variable (measurement).

External validity, another process related to experimental research, deals with whether a researcher can generalize his or her research. In fact, all studies to some extent are limited in terms of external validity. The following paragraph discusses face validity.

Simply stated, **face validity** is simply the appearance on its face that an instrument has items that measure what they are supposed to measure. This form of validity does not address if items from an instrument actually measure what they purport or suppose to measure. The next section addresses another nonstatistical form of validity referred to as content validity.

CONTENT VALIDITY

Lyman (1997) used several terms such as **logical validity**, **course validity**, **curricular validity**, and **textbook validity** to describe content validity. Even though content validity is more systematic and sophisticated than face validity, or the superficial appearance or looks of validity, it is still nonstatistical or nonquantitative. Bryant (2000) defined content validity as the degree to which items from an instrument assess relevant aspects of the conceptual domain in which the items from the instrument were intended to measure. As Bryant correctly stated, domains can be behavioral. For example, if one were interested in measuring high school mathematical ability, one would want items that tap into the domains that are generally covered for high school mathematics, such as algebra, geometry, trigonometry, and so on; however, if one failed to sample a relevant domain—quadratic equations—it could be argued that the items for the high school mathematical instrument lacked relevant content validity. Often, a table of specification can help one determine relevant domains for a test and the percentage of items that may be needed to represent a domain. Moreover, experts' judgments and the analysis of the content of a test can help establish content validity. Clearly, content validity is important for achievement tests and certain occupational tests, but it may not be appropriate for certain personality and ability tests (Sapp, 2014).

CRITERION VALIDITY

Criterion validity is a statistical form of validity, with at least three forms (predictive, concurrent, and retrospective), that is sometimes referred to as empirical validity. **Criterion validity** tells us if the items that form the criterion, say from two tests, correlate. And the correlation for items from two tests is called a **validity coefficient**. Lyman (1997) noted that generally **validity coefficients** fall between **.20** and **.60**, depending on the items obtained from a particular test. Often, validity coefficients between **.30** to **.40** are acceptable for many situations. Unlike reliability coefficients, validity coefficients must be squared to determine the variance accounted for; variance accounted for is called the **coefficient of determination**; to illustrate, a validity coefficient of .5 indicates that .25 or 25% of the variance can be explained or accounted for, and 75% of the variance remains unexplained. In summary, validity coefficients represent unsquared area, while reliability coefficients represent squared area. The reader may have inferred that the correlation between two sets of scores could represent reliability or validity, because the representation is determined by the purpose of the clinician or researcher; however, often with reliability, the two sets of scores are correlated for the same test. In contrast, often with validity, one set of scores from one test are correlated with criterion values of another test. The following section describes predictive validity.

PREDICTIVE VALIDITY

Predictive validity is a form of criterion validity, and it is also known as **prospective validity**. As the name suggests, predictive validity has a future connotation to assess this form of validity. A clinician or researcher must obtain predictor test scores (**predictor-independent variables, covariates, or pretests**) before measuring the criterion or dependent measure or variables. A validity coefficient can be found for predictive validity by correlating predictor scores with the criteria scores. Bryant (2000) recommends multiple regression as a means to calculate predictive validity. **Multiple regression** is multivariate technique that uses several predictors (pretest, covariates, or before measures) to predict a criterion. A theme that has been emphasized within this book is that many data analytical techniques are special cases of structural equation modeling, and the same applies to multiple regression analysis. The reader is recommended to consult Sapp (2006) and Pituch and Stevens (2016) for a discussion of multiple regression analysis, but this writer as well as Thompson (1995) do not support the use of stepwise regression or stepwise discriminant analysis, unless scores have been factor analyzed and the factor scores are passed into a regression analysis. The reader can read the section within Sapp (2006) on exploratory factor analysis using SPSS, where scores are factor analyzed and passed into a regression equation.

Descriptive discriminant analysis is a form of regression designed for classifying or discriminating group membership. For example, descriptive discriminant analysis could be used to determine customers who are low or high credit risks (two categories low and high credit risk). Thompson found that the statistical packages used to calculate these analyses, stepwise regression and stepwise discriminant analysis, calculated the total degrees of freedom correctly, namely n-1 (the number of participants minus one), but the degrees of freedom for explained, model, regression, between is computed as the number of entered predictor variables. Because of the preceding statistical packages error, the degrees of freedom for unexplained, error, residual, or within is then computed as n-1-pv, where pv is the number of predictor variables. These errors, which are performed by statistical packages, lead to F calculated values, where F is just a statistic that is used to test the statistical significance of stepwise regression and stepwise discriminant analysis. Readers may be assuming that regression is not ever appropriate; however, regression is appropriate when the clinician or researcher selects the order of entry of predictors into a regression equation, and do not leave the selection to statistical packages. Moreover, if a reader decides on using regression as a validity or data analytic technique, consult Thompson and Borrello (1985) who recommend using structure coefficients in addition to standardized beta weights when interpreting regression analyses.

Structure coefficients, or **structure correlations,** also called **loadings**, are not affected by multicolinearity, the intercorrelation of predictors, like standardized beta weights. The structure coefficients are widely used with several multivariate techniques, such as **descriptive discriminant analysis** and **canonical correlation**. By definition, **a structure coefficient**, also called factor loadings, is the correlation of a predictor with a dependent variable divided by the multiple regression correlation (R) for the entire regression equation (Vogt, 1999; Vogt & Johnson, 2011). Pedhazur (1997) noted that when standardized beta weights have substantive meaning from a regression analysis, structure coefficients greater than or equal to .30 can be treated as meaningful. In summary, structure coefficients, as Pedhazur noted, are zero order (correlation of one x variable and one y variable) divided by a constant, the multiple correlation coefficient. Unlike Thompson and Borrello, within the regression context, Pedhazur does not believe that structure coefficients aid in the interpretation.

Returning to predictive validity, it is strongest when the testing process does not affect the criterion (Bryant, 2000). Also, this writer agrees with Bryant in emphasizing that structural equation modeling is the most powerful multivariate technique to assess predictive validity. An issue related to predictive validity is differential validity, or the process where a predictor or set of predictors predict scores on a criterion differently for different subgroups. **Differential validity** can exist when subgroups (blacks vs. white participants) differ on slopes, y intercepts, or standard errors. Differential validity can be problematic in the workplace where there can be validity coefficients differences across racial groups. The next section addresses concurrent validity.

Concurrent validity is where a clinician or researcher obtains predictor (pretests, covariates, etc.) and criterion measures at the same point in time. When the two sets of scores are correlated, the result is a concurrent validity coefficient. If the two measures can be collected independently of the participants, there results are stronger.

The last form of criterion validity is **retrospective** or **postdictive** validity, and it is the weakest form of criterion validity. **Retrospective validity** attempts to determine if test scores correlate with a criterion measure that focuses on the past; hence, this is postdictive validity. Sometimes clinicians or researchers can locate archival records to quantify criterions measurements found at an earlier period of time (Bryant, 2000).

We will close our discussion of criterion validity by summarizing several factors that affect this form of validity. **First**, test items chosen from a predictor variable and criterion variable may differ so much that they are not comparable. And as Lyman (1997) indicated, sometimes a predictor is a better measure of a characteristic than the criterion itself. **Second**, as previously stated, groups can differ. For example, a criterion-related validity may work well for Group A, but it may be ineffective for another group—Group B. **Third**, just as large amounts of variability increase reliability, a similar occurrence happens with validity coefficients, the greater the variability—chances are the validity coefficient will be larger, especially when compared with a homogenous group of participants. Finally, as Lyman stated, criterion or empirical validity must be evaluated in terms of how much additional information is provided. In summary, criterion-related validity is a form of **empirical validity** that only differs in time sequences that are predictive, concurrent, or retrospective.

CONSTRUCT VALIDITY

Factorial or **structural validity** is a form of validity related to content validity and construct validity, and it can be assessed by determining the number of factors, structures, or dimensions that underlie a set of items from a test. **Principal components analysis**, **factor analysis**, and **confirmatory factor analysis**, all of which are a special case of structural equations modeling, a multivariate procedure, can determine factorial, structural, or construct validity. Principal components analysis analyzes the correlation among variables with 1s on the main diagonal of a correlation matrix, and as Kahn (2006) stated, it analyzes all the variance among variables. In contrast, factor analysis, or principal-axis factoring, analyzes the correlation among variables in a correlation matrix with communalities on the main diagonal of a correlation matrix. In contrast to principal components analysis, principal-axis factoring assumes that latent factors underlie the observed variables. Vogt (1999) defined **communality** as the amount or proportion of total variance that two or factors share, common factor variance. In terms of a calculation, it is often denoted as h^2, which is the sum of the squared factor loadings or the correlations between each variable and each factor (Vogt). Factor loadings are analogous to regression coefficients or slopes, and loadings less than .30 or .40 are not viewed as meaningful.

Table 1.2 has factor loadings. Notice that Variable 1 has a .20 with Factor I, and it has a .80 loading with Factor II. Table 1.2 has the squared loading and commonalities. Note that the squared loading for Variable 2 with Factor II is .04 and with Factor II .64. And the communalities (h^2) for Variables 3 and 4 are .58 and .68, respectively. Another way of viewing the communality of a variable is as the squared multiple correlation or covariance with a factor. Because communalities are **squared multiple correlations**, this puts them within squared area world like reliabilities, and by definition reliability can be defined as a **communality plus specificity**, where specificity is the variance due to factors specific to the test items. Moreover, communality indicates the proportion of variance accounted by all for a given variable. Furthermore, communalities are **lower-bounds** or lower estimates of reliability; like coefficient alpha. This means that the population reliability will not be lower than a communality or coefficient alpha, but it can be larger.

Table 1.1
LOADINGS

	Factor I	Factor II
Variable 1	.20	.80
Variable 2	.20	.80
Variable 3	.30	.70
Variable 4	.80	.20
Variable 5	.80	.10
Variable 6	.80	.20

Table 1.2
SQUARED LOADINGS AND COMMONALITIES

	Factor I	Factor II	h^2
Variable 1	.04	.64	$.68 = h^2$
Variable 2	.04	.64	$.68 = h^2$
Variable 3	.09	.49	$.58 = h^2$
Variable 4	.64	.04	$.68 = h^2$
Variable 5	.64	.01	$.65 = h^2$
Variable 6	.64	.04	$.68 = h^2$

Pituch and Stevens (2016) noted that both factor analysis and principal components analysis often produce the same results, and this writer prefers principal components analysis because it is simpler mathematically than factor analysis. The type of principal components analysis I am discussing is called exploratory, because we are attempting to determine how many constructs or factors (correlated or uncorrelated) underlie a given set of data, and, often, we wish to name the factors (Thompson, 2004). In contrast, confirmatory factor analysis, is based on strong theoretical and/or empirical evidence, and the clinician or researcher knows or has an idea how many factors underlie a set of data and if the factors are correlated or uncorrelated. Moreover, the clinician or researcher attempts, with confirmatory factor analysis, to confirm a hypothesized factor structure for a set of data.

Pituch and Stevens (2016) defines principal components, mathematically, as a multivariate technique that partitions total variance by finding a linear combination of the variables that accounts for the maximum amount of variance. The linear combination of variables for principal components analysis can be represented by the following equation:

$$y1 = a11\ x1 + a12\ x2 + \ldots + a1pxp$$

y_1 is the first principal component, and if a_{11}, a_{12} … a_1p—the coefficients are scaled such that $\mathbf{a'_1}\ \mathbf{a_1} = 1$. The reader should note that the expression $\mathbf{a'_1}\ \mathbf{a_1}$ is the product of two matrices in the following form:

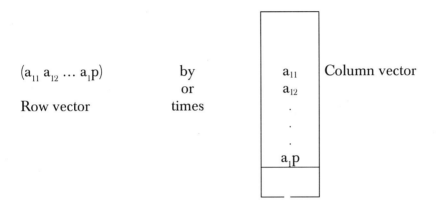

Now the variance of y_1 equals the largest eigenvalue, the sum of the squared loadings on a factor, of the sample covariance matrix (Pituch & Stevens, 2016). Furthermore, the coefficients $a_{11}\ a_{12}\ \ldots\ a_1p$ are the elements of the eigenvector, denoted as $(a_{11}\ a_{12}\ \ldots\ a_1p)$, correspond to the largest eigenvalue. After the first principal component is found, the second linear combination of variables that accounts for the next largest amount of variance is found. The reader should note these components are uncorrelated, and the equation for the second principal component is:

$$y_2 = a_{21}\ x_1 + a_{22}\ x_2 \ldots a_{2p}x_p.$$

The coefficients $(a_{22}\ x_2\ \ldots\ a_{2p}x_p)$ are scaled such that $\mathbf{a'_2}\ \mathbf{a_2}$ equals one. The reader should notice that the correlation between y_1 and y_2 equals zero. This indicates the lack of correlation of factors; hence, principal components analysis is a statistical way of handling multicollinearity (the correlation of predictors). And as Pituch and Stevens noted, the coefficients of the second component are the elements of the eigenvector with the second largest eigenvalue of the covariance matrix; therefore, the sample variance of y_2 equals the second largest eigenvalue. This iterative process continues calculating linear components until no variance is left; thus, principal components analysis is a **mathematical maximization procedure**; that is, proceeding components maximize the amount of variance remaining; hence, components accounts for the maximum amount of variance that is possible.

Probably the most controversial and the most interesting form of validity is construct-related validity. **Construct validity** helps determine if a given measurement instrument actually assesses or measures the underlying conceptual construct which it was designed to measure (Bryant, 2000). Construct validity is not a fixed construct, meaning that clinicians and researchers can assess it whenever data are collected. And it takes several studies and an overwhelming body of evidence provided by a variety of sources to establish and maintain construct validity. Often, clinicians and researchers will consult a test manual for an instrument and assume that the reported construct validity measure or measures are fixed, but as it has been repeatedly emphasized that psychometric properties are not fixed, however, they are merely a function of measured test items that can vary from sample to sample.

Convergent and discriminant validity are the two major forms of construct validity. First, **convergent validity** is the degree to which several measures appear to measure the same construct, and the measures are said to converge or agree. For example, instruments that are designed to measure psychological trauma should all be intercorrelated, and the more similar the instrument, the higher the correlations should be among the instruments. The reader should notice that again correlation coefficients are used to assess validity–in this case construct validity. In contrast, with **discriminant validity**, because multiple measures of distinct constructs are different, items from the multiple measures should not have high correlations.

Bryant (2000) described the **multitrait-multimethod** as a powerful means to assess convergent and discriminant validity. This method consists of a correlation matrix between two or more theoretical constructs–for example, two measures of depression, with each construct measured or assessed by two or more methods. The multitrait-multimethod matrix can assess if scores obtained are the result of the trait measured or the methods of measurement.

EFFECT SIZES

Effect sizes are seldom reported within research. Effect sizes allow researchers to determine if results have practical significance, and they allow one to determine the degree of effect a treatment has within a population; or simply stated, the degree in which the null hypothesis may be false. There are over 40 different effect sizes, but, as I discussed within the history of effect size section, that they can be grouped into two broad areas means differences effect sizes like the d effect size and correlational effect sizes like effect size r (Ferguson, 2009).

Cohen (1977) defined the most basic effect measure, the statistic that is synthesized, as an analog to the t-tests for means. Specifically, for a two-group situation, he defined the d effect size as the differences between two population means divided by the standard deviation of either population, because homogeneity or equality of variances is assumed. This effect size has the general formula:

$$d = \frac{\mu_1 - \mu_2}{\sigma}$$

μ_1 = the treatment group
μ_2 = the control group
σ = population standard deviation

Suppose μ_1 equals the population mean, and in this case we are using it to represent the treatment group population mean of 1.0. And let us assume that μ_2, the population mean for the control group, equals .2, and, finally, $\sigma = 1.00$. By substitution,

$$d = \frac{1.0 - .2}{1} = 8$$

Hedges' g or d is Cohen's d[1-(3/4df-1)] The df is the total sample size minus two. Now, this formula can create confusion because different effect sizes can be found for the same data. For example, the σ or population standard deviation can be from the control group posttest measure. In addition, it can be the pretest standard deviation for the control group, or it can be the pooled or weighted standard deviation that involves both groups. Therefore, within a study, at least three different d effect sizes can be obtained. First, one based on the control group posttest measure standard deviation. Second, another based on the control group pretest measure, and a d effect size measure based on the average standard deviation for the treatment and control group.

As stated early, actually, the differences between means divided by the control group standard deviation is Glass's delta and not the specific d that Cohen proposed, but many researchers assume that all ds are Cohen's ds. The d that Cohen proposed was the differences between two group means divided by the pool standard deviations of the treatment group and control group. Cohen's d assumed homogeneity of variances. If this assumption is violated, one would want to choose which standard deviation to use because they cannot be pooled. With repeated measures designs, it can be argued that it does not make sense to calculate Cohen's d. This is because Cohen's d was developed for independent groups. One can use eta squared with repeated measures designs. In practice, many researchers, for Cohen's d, find the differences between the treatment and control groups means divided by the average of the standard deviation of the treatment group and the standard deviation of the control group. Cohen's d is upwardly biased, and this is why Hedges developed his d to take into account this biased. Cohen's d is more appropriate for population data while Hedges' d is more appropriate for sample data. These d effect sizes from several studies can be averaged, and the result is an overall effect size for a series of studies. Meta-analysis is just the overall effect for a given area or mean effect size, and it is obtained by adding the effects sizes and dividing by the total number (Ferguson, 2007). Also, effect sizes are used for statistical power analysis, or the probability of rejecting a false null hypothesis.

Although Cohen (1977) provided the following rough guidelines for interpreting the d effect size: $d = .2$ small effect size, $d = .5$ medium effect size, and $d = .8$ large effect size, researchers should not interpret blindly effect sizes as small, medium, and large. One must interpret effect sizes within a given professional area.

There is another effect size called r, and it was described by Rosenthal (1984). The reader may remember that r is the Pearson product-moment correlation coefficient. Mathematically, r is the covariance, the amount two variables vary co-varies, divided by the number of pairs times the product of the standard deviation for each variable. The following is the formula for the Pearson product-moment correlation:

$$r = \frac{\Sigma Z_x Z_y}{N}.$$

Here, Z_x is every X value minus the mean of the X values divided by the standard deviation of the X values. Similarly, Z_y is every Y value minus the mean of the Y values divided by the standard deviation of the Y values. Z_x and Z_y are analogous to standard deviation and are referred to as moments, hence the name Pearson Product-Moment Correlation. The reader should note that a moment is a measure of variability like the standard deviation. Like Cohen (1977), Rosenthal provided the following rough guidelines for r: $r = .1$ small effect size, $r = .3$ medium effect size, and $r = .5$ large effect size. The following section will describe a common multivariate effect size that is analogous to the d effect size. The next section discusses a multivariate generalization of the d effect size for two independent groups.

DEFINITIONS OF MULTIVARIATE STATISTICS

The term multivariate can be a confusing term, but in one sense, it involves examining several variables simultaneously. Within a regression context, it is the relationship between two or more predictors (independent variables) and a dependent variable. From a multivariate regression context, it involves the relationship between two or more predictors and two or more dependent variables. Other multivariate correlation methods are path analysis, factor analysis, principal components analysis, canonical correlation, and predictive discriminant analysis (Pituch & Stevens 2016).

When two or more groups of participants are measured on several dependent variables, this is a multivariate analysis of variance (MANOVA), a multivariate extension of ANOVA. Multivariate analysis of covariance (MANCOVA), a multivariate generalization of ANCOVA, step down analysis, a multivariate test procedure that focuses on the ordering of dependent variables through a series of analyses of covariance, and descriptive discriminant analysis, a multivariate technique that determines group membership, and log linear analysis, an extension of the chi-square test to three or more variables are all examples of multivariate statistics. In summary, if participants are measured on two or more dependent variables, a multivariate situation exists.

Why are multivariate statistics important? First, they control type I error, but with many univariate tests it cannot be easily estimated.

Second, univariate statistics do not consider, or take into account, the correlations among variables. Finally, multivariate statistics are more powerful statistically than univariate statistics.

Hotelling's T squared is the squared multivariate generalization of the t test. The univariate t test is the following:

Hoteling's T² is the following:

$$t = \frac{\overline{y}_1 - \overline{y}_2}{\sqrt{\frac{(n_1-1)s_1^2 + (n_2-1)s_2^2}{n_1+n_2-2}\left(\frac{1}{n_1}+\frac{1}{n_2}\right)}}$$

$$T^2 = \frac{n_1 n_2}{n_1 + n_2}(\overline{\mathbf{y}}_1 - \overline{\mathbf{y}}_2)' \mathbf{S}^{-1}(\overline{\mathbf{y}}_1 - \overline{\mathbf{y}}_2)$$

$(\overline{\mathbf{y}}_1 - \overline{\mathbf{y}}_2)'$ transpose of vector of means

S - sample covariance matrix

$\mathbf{S}^{-1}$ matrix analogue of division is inversion

$(\overline{\mathbf{y}}_1 - \overline{\mathbf{y}}_2)$ vectors of means

The connection between Hotelling's T² and F is the following:

$$F = \frac{n_1 + n_2 - p - 1}{(n_1 + n_2 - 2)p} T^2$$

This formula shows that T² provides a F distribution with p and (N-P-1) degrees of freedom. The p is the number of dependent variables and N equals the sample size. Essentially, T² is the comparison of between variability divided by within variability.

The univariate d and Mahalanobis distance (D²) are the following:

univariate   multivariate

$$d = \frac{\overline{y}_1 - \overline{y}_2}{s} \qquad D^2 = (\overline{\mathbf{y}}_1 - \overline{\mathbf{y}}_2)' \mathbf{S}^{-1}(\overline{\mathbf{y}}_1 - \overline{\mathbf{y}}_2)$$

D^2 is also the following two formulas:

This is formula one. $[(n_1 + n_2)/n_1 n_2] T^2$

This is formula two.

$$\frac{1}{1-r^2}\left[\frac{(x_{i1} - \bar{x}_1)^2}{s_1^2} + \frac{(x_{i2} - \bar{x}_2)^2}{s_2^2} - \frac{2r(x_{i1} - \bar{x}_1)(x_{i2} - \bar{x}_2)}{s_1 s_2}\right]$$

Formula two, clearly shows how D^2 takes into account the correlation of these variables.

And T^2 is the following:

$$[n_1 n_2 /(n_1 + n_2)] D^2$$

Pituch and Stevens (2016) stated that values of .25 are small effect sizes, values of .5 are medium effect sizes, and values greater than one are large effect sizes. Unlike univariate statistics, Mahalanobis distance takes into account the intercorrelation of variables. Readers can refer to Sapp, Obiakor, Gregas, and Scholze (2007) and Pituch and Stevens (2016) on how to calculate Mahalanobis statistic with SPSS.

CONFIDENCE INTERVALS

Ferguson (2009) and Sapp (2004a 2004b) defined a confidence interval as an interval among an infinite number of intervals for a parameter such as population mean, population reliability coefficient, population proportion, population correlation coefficient, population difference, and so on, in which one minus the alpha level would capture the population parameter a certain percentage of the time. For example, for a population mean, 95% of these intervals would capture the population mean and 5% would not. In contrast to point estimates, which describe sample data, confidence intervals describe population characteristics. More specifically, confidence intervals allow researchers to put a lower limit and upper limit around a population parameter. The 95% and 99% are most used intervals, but any interval width can be established. For the 99% interval, a researcher is assuming that 99%

of these intervals capture these population parameters, and 1% would not. Clearly, a 99 percent interval is wider than a 95 percent one (Sapp, Obiakor, Scholze, & Gregas, 2007; Sapp, 2004a; Thompson, 2002; Sapp 2002).

Confidence intervals can be placed around IQ and other standardized scores. For example, the Wechsler Adults Intelligence Scale (WAIS), a commonly used measure of intelligence, has a standard error of measurement of 5. Since the standard error of measurement is interpreted in terms of the normal curve, confidence intervals can be formed around IQ scores. For example, if an African American student had an IQ score of 100 on the WAIS, this IQ scores of 100 plus and minus one times the standard error approximates the 68% confidence interval. The IQ score of 100 minus the standard error of five equals 95, which is the lower limit. And the IQ score of 100 plus 5 equals the upper limit. This means we can expect this African American student's true IQ score to fall between 95 and 105 68% of the time. Similarly, 100 plus and minus 1.96 times the standard error of measurement (5) represents the 95% confidence interval. Finally, 100 plus and minus 2.58 times the standard error of measurement forms the 99% confidence interval.

TESTING CALCULATED VALIDITY COEFFICIENTS AGAINST HYPOTHESIZED VALUES

Just as values of reliability can be tested against hypothesized values, the same test can be performed with validity coefficients. Two independent validity coefficients can be tested for statistical significance using the following Z-test (Sapp, 1997):

$$Z = \frac{Zr_1 - Zr_2}{\left(\frac{1}{N_1 - 3} + \frac{1}{N_2 - 3}\right)^{1/2}}$$

Zr_1 and Zr_2 are Fisher's z transformations of r for the validity coefficients. Suppose that sample one had a validity coefficient or index $r_1 = .50$, with 100 participants and sample had a validity coefficient or $r_2 = .35$, also with 100 participants. The first step is to find the Fisher's z transformation for each validity coefficient, and these values are found in Table 1. For $r_1 = .50$, the Fisher's z is $Zr_1 = .549$, and for $r_2 = .35$, the Fisher's z is .365. Substituting into the formula:

$$Z = \frac{.549 - .365}{\left(\frac{1}{97} + \frac{1}{97}\right)^{\frac{1}{2}}} = \frac{.184}{(.010309278 + .010309278)^{\frac{1}{2}}}$$

$$= \frac{.184}{.143591631} = 1.281411732 \text{ or } 1.28 \text{ at 2 decimal places.}$$

Because Z of 1.28 is not greater than a Z of 1.96 (critical value), the validity coefficients are not statistically significantly different. Finally, for two related or correlated validity coefficients, the formula is the following:

$$Z = \frac{Zr_1 - Zr_2}{\left(\frac{1}{N-3}\right)^{\frac{1}{2}}}$$

Using the validity coefficients, suppose that a population validity coefficient of .50 exists within some bivariate normal distribution, and suppose a random sample of 100 participants were drawn randomly from the normal population distribution and the sample validity coefficient is .35. Substituting into the formula provides the following:

$$Z = \frac{.549 - .365}{\left(\frac{1}{97}\right)^{\frac{1}{2}}} = \frac{.184}{(.010309278)^{\frac{1}{2}}}$$

$$= \frac{.184}{.101534617} = 1.812189836 \text{ or } 1.81 \text{ rounded to two decimal places.}$$

Again, since the calculated value of Z of 1.81 is not greater than the critical value of Z, which is 1.96, the two related validity coefficients are not statistically significantly different. The next section discusses a concept related to validity called the standard error of estimate. One can do a Google search and find many random number generators that can be used for random assignment and random sample selection.

STANDARD ERROR OF ESTIMATE

The standard error of estimate is to validity what the standard error of measurement is to reliability, and the standard error of estimate is associated with criterion validity. When a predictor is used to predict a criterion, there is error in measurement or prediction. The standard error of estimate is the standard deviation of the predictor errors, and it provides a range in which a client's score will fall, given a client's score on a test. The formula for the standard error of estimate is as follows:

$$SE_{est} = S_y = \sqrt{1 - r_{xy}^2}$$

SE_{est} = the standard error of estimate

S_y = the standard deviation of the criterion scores

r_{xy} = the validity coefficient

Confidence intervals can be established for the standard error of estimate, just like the ones used with the standard error of measurement.

CONFIDENCE INTERVALS AROUND VALIDITY

Confidence intervals can be placed around validity. As previously stated, validity is the correlation among a set of items that been shown to be valid with a set of items being tested to determine their validity; therefore, validity can be defined as a simple correlation. The sampling distribution of the Pearson product-moment correlation, the most commonly used one, is skewed; therefore, this correlation must be turned into a logarithmic transformation. The reader can see Sapp (2006) for these transformations. Suppose, a researcher had a validity coefficient of .30 for a hypnosis study, how could one construct a 95% confidence interval around the population validity coefficient? First, turn the validity coefficient into its logarithmic transformation that is .31. Suppose this validity coefficient is based on 25 cases. Like the reliability example, we need the standard error, which is one divided by the square root of the number of cases minus three; therefore, the standard error is .21. The 95% confidence interval is .31 plus and minus 1.96 times .21, so the lower limit is -.10 and the upper limit is .72. We have to transform these logarithmic values back to regular correlations, and these become -.10 for the lower limit and .62 for the upper limit. The reader should notice the confidence interval -.10, .62 contains zero; therefore, the population correlation coefficient does not differ significantly from zero; therefore, there is not statistical significance.

With centralized distributions, such as the normal curve and t-distribution for centralized cases, confidence intervals are straightforward. For example, the confidence interval for the one-sample t-test is the sample mean plus and minus the critical value of the t test statistics times the standard error. For the two-sample t-test case, the sample mean is replaced with the difference between means. For example, the formula for the confidence interval for a two-sample t-test is the following: $(\overline{X}_1 - \overline{X}_2) \pm (t)$ (standard error). Again, X bars are the sample means and t is the t test statistic.

The t formula is the following:

$$t = \frac{\overline{X}_1 - \overline{X}_2}{\sqrt{\frac{S_1^2}{N_1} + \frac{S_2^2}{N_2}}}$$

The Ss squared are the standard deviations of each group squared and the Ns are the sample sizes for each group. Confidence intervals can be placed around validity indices or correlation indices and multiple squared correlations (Sapp, 2006; Steiger & Fouladi, 1997; Smithson, 2003). As previously stated, before a confidence interval can be establish, one must determine if one is working with a centralized or noncentalized distribution. The reason the normal curve is centralized is because it has a population mean of zero and a standard deviation of one. The centralized t-distribution is a generalization of the normal distribution, and it is defined by a mean of zero and degrees of freedom. Noncentalized distributions are defined by their degrees of freedom and noncentalized parameters.

The upper and lower limits for a confidence interval for a one-sample case are found by finding the mean plus and minus the critical value of the t test statistics times the standard error. The minus part of this definition provides the lower limit and the plus part provides the upper limit. The following is an example of a one-sample case with a 95 percent confidence interval.

A PRACTICAL EXAMPLE OF A ONE SAMPLE CASE 95% CONFIDENCE INTERVAL

Assume that a university tested a random sample of ten students on the SAT, and the population mean was 708. The following are these students' SAT scores:

> 708
> 707
> 710
> 708
> 711
> 707
> 708
> 710
> 707
> 709

Calculate the appropriate test statistic for this design. Is the test statistic significant? Calculate a 95% confidence interval.

One-Sample Test

	Test Value = 708					
					95% Confidence Interval of the Difference	
	T	df	Sig. (2-tailed)	Mean Difference	Lower	Upper
SAT Score	1.103	9	.299	.50000	-.5256	1.5256

The appropriate test statistic for this design is the one-sample t-test, and statistical significance was not obtained because the level of significance or probability value was .299 for the t-test statistic; a value of .05 or lower is needed for statistical significance. The reader should notice that the 95% confidence interval of the difference between the sample mean and population mean has a lower limit of -.5256 and upper limit of 1.5256. Since zero is included within the interval, a statistical significance difference was not found between the sample mean and the population mean. These upper and lower limits are found by taking the mean difference (sample mean of 708.5-705 =.50) plus and minus the critical value of t which is 2.262 times the standard error which is .45338. The mean difference of .50 plus 1.02554556 equals 1.5256 rounded to four decimal places. In contrast, the mean difference of .50 minus 1.02554556 equals -.5256 rounded to four decimal places. This suggests that the sample mean is representative of the population mean. The confidence interval for the one-sample case t-test equals the mean plus and minus the critical value of t times the standard error of the mean. If the population mean is not known, the sample mean alone is used to find the confidence interval. Again, the critical value of t for nine degrees of freedom is 2.262; therefore, the upper limit for this confidence interval is 708.5+2.262(.45338). 2.262(.45338)=1.02554556.

708.5+1.02554556=709.5255456   upper limit
708.5-1.02554556=707.4744544   lower limit

Finally, we are 95% confidence that the mean SAT score of all these students lies between 707.5 to 709.5, and the sample value of 708 is representative of the population parameter. In summary, point estimates such as 708 describes a sample, and confidence intervals tell us what happens in the population and is an estimate of the population parameter. In essence, it provides an estimate of the mean SAT score for all these students (population). The following is the general formula for a centralized confidence interval: $\overline{X} \pm (t)(\text{Standard Error})$. X bar is the mean, and t is the critical value of t for the desired confidence interval, and the standard error is found by finding the standard deviation divided by the square root of the number of scores.

Confidence intervals for coefficient alpha involve noncentralized distribution. Let us take the example we used before for coefficient alpha. What is the 95% confidence interval around the population coefficient alpha?

The SPSS control lines for this example are the following:

```
RELIABILITY
  /VARIABLES=item1 item2 item3 item4 item5 item6
  /SCALE('ALL VARIABLES')  ALL/MODEL=ALPHA
  /STATISTICS=DESCRIPTIVE SCALE CORR ANOVA
  /ICC=MODEL(MIXED) TYPE(CONSISTENCY) CIN=95
    TESTVAL=0.
```

These results for the 95% confidence interval around coefficient alpha were .308 for the lower limit and .897 for the upper limit. Remember from the earlier example, the .691 tells us what happens with the sample data and is referred to as a sample measure of internal consistency. The 95% confidence interval captures the parameter called the population coefficient alpha, and it means that over repeated samples of confidence intervals, 95% of the intervals will captures the parameter called the population coefficient alpha, and 5% of the intervals will not capture the population coefficient alpha. The 5% chance that values can fall outside of the interval suggests that over repeated samples, 2.5% of the intervals will be too low and 2.5% will be too high. In summary, the confidence interval around coefficient alpha deals with the population coefficient alpha that will be represented through several samples or repeated sampling.

It is possible to test a coefficient alpha against a specified value. For example, does a value of .59 differ from the alpha obtained with our coefficient alpha of .691? The SPSS codes for running this analysis are the following:

```
RELIABILITY
 /VARIABLES=trial1 trial2 trial3 trial4 trial5 trial6
 /SCALE('ALL VARIABLES')  ALL/MODEL=ALPHA
 /STATISTICS=ANOVA
 /ICC=MODEL(MIXED) TYPE(CONSISTENCY) CIN=95
 TESTVAL=.59
```

Results from the F test for the average measures reported an F value of 1.325, p=.236. This indicated that the two values were not statistically significantly different from each other. Testing coefficient alpha against a specific value is an advancement beyond null hypothesis testing. Readers can see Thompson (2003) for a thorough discussion of this advancement in measurement. Finally, confidence intervals can be found for the d effect sizes and other noncentralized measures such as coefficient alpha.

DISCUSSION

This section addressed three major areas important for research, and areas were the following: measurement, effect sizes, and confidence intervals. Measurement is important for understanding research. As previously stated, minorities are seldom included within psychological research. There are over 40 different measures of effect and some are standardized differences like Cohen's d or in correlation form like r. Finally, effect sizes can be presented as corrected and uncorrected measures.

Thompson (1994;2003) has made many recommendations for social sciences research, and this writer thinks the same applies to counseling psychology research. He recommended that researchers put confidence intervals around reliabilities like coefficient alpha. As stated within this article, reliability is a function of test items and reliability measures the consistency of test items. Also, as previously stated, a confidence interval is an interval among an infinitely large set of intervals for a given parameter in which 95% of the intervals would capture the population parameter.

Confidence intervals around reliability indices require a non-centralized distribution – which allows one to a perform power analysis, or the probability of rejecting a false null hypothesis (no treatment effect). Also, this distribution is not centered at zero. The SPSS computer software was used to calculate non-centralized distributions for reliabilities. Unlike centralized distributions, which have a mean of zero, a non-centralized distribution has a mean of some hypothesized value, and non-centralized distributions are skewed (Bird, 2002). As demonstrated within this chapter, confidence intervals were placed around reliability and validity indices. It should be clear to readers, in order to construct a confidence interval, one must know the distribution that one is working with such as normal, centralized t-distribution and so on. Confidence intervals allow one to test statistical significance and to find what happens in the population. In contrast, traditional significance testing only allows one to reject or fail to reject the null hypothesis.

The author has challenged the use of null hypothesis statistical significance testing within these social sciences (Sapp, 2015; 2006). Readers should be aware that null hypothesis statistical significance testing only allows one to determine if a relationship is significantly greater than zero, and it does not ensure replication, nor does it control for threats to internal validity.

Internal validity is the judgment applied by a researcher to determine if an independent variable caused a change on a dependent variable, of if a treatment, drug, or intervention actually made a difference.

Theoretically, random assignment or randomly assigning participants to groups initially controls for all threats to internal validity.

Sapp (2015) recommended that researchers provide effect size measures and reliability indices for their data. In addition, he recommended confidence intervals for d effect size measures. Unfortunately, this process is an iterative one that involves non-central distributions and readers who are interested in SPSS programs for calculating such intervals can consult Bird (2002) and Smithson (2003). Professor Geoff Cumming, at La Trobe University in Australia, has developed software that runs under the Excel program, which can be downloaded by doing a Google search. This software calculates confidence intervals for these d effect size measures.

Finally, researchers need to provide effect size measures for their data, and that they need to calculate reliability indices for their data. In conclusion, researchers need to think meta-analytically, and not mindlessly apply statistics and measurement (Fidler, Cumming, Thomason, Pannuzzo, Smith, Fyffe et al., 2005).

THE EFFECT SIZE R

The effect size r is a correlation coefficient. This statistic was introduced when we discussed reliability, a squared correlation coefficient, and validity, an unsquared correlation coefficient. The effect size r is the relationship or association between an independent variable, denoted by "x," and a dependent variable, denoted by "y." Moreover, the effect size r can be the correlation of a pretest or covariate and a dependent variable or posttest measure.

Effect sizes allow researchers to determine if a relationship has practical significance. Traditional statistical tests such as t-test, F-test, and chi square only allow one to determine if a relationship is significantly greater than zero. In other words, traditional statistical tests permit one to reject or fail to reject the null hypothesis, no treatment effect, or the population means are not significantly different, but effect sizes allow one to determine the degree of effect a treatment has within a population, or the degree in which the null hypothesis may be false.

The r effect size, also called Pearson Product-Moment Correlation, measures a linear relationship between two variables. Quasi-interval data or higher is assumed with the r effect size. Quasi-intervals are obtained from data when equal differences among measurements represent the same or equal amount of difference. For example, the difference between 80° F (Fahrenheit) and 90° F is an equal distance of 10° F. Most standardized tests are quasi-interval data.

The Pearson r is another name for the effect size r, and it communicates two bits of information. First, it gives the magnitude of the relationship between two linearly related variables. The larger the size of the correlation, the greater the magnitude; however, the maximum magnitude for the effect size r coefficient can have is +1.00 or -1.00. Second, the effect size r tells us the direction of the relationship. For example, an r effect size of +1.00 indicates a perfect, positive relationship between an independent variable and dependent variable. Specifically, as the independent variable increases, the corresponding dependent variable increases. In contrast, an r of -1.00 indicates a perfect negative relationship between the independent and dependent variables with a perfect negative r effect size. As the independent variable increases, the corresponding dependent variable decreases. The reader should note that it is arbitrary which variable is called independent or dependent, because the effect size r is a symmetrical correlation. This means that the correlation of X and Y equals the correlation of Y and X.

Verbally, the formula for the r effect size is the mean of the product of z-scores. In other words, we find the z scores for all X and Y scores and then multiply every X and Y pair, and we add the product (multiplication) of every corresponding X and Y z-score and divide by the total number of pairs. This simple formula is expressed as:

$$r = \frac{\Sigma Z_x Z_y}{N}$$

Here, Z_x is every X value minus the mean of the X values divided by the standard deviation of the X values. Similarly, Z_y is every Y value minus the mean of the Y values divided by the standard deviation of the Y values. Z_x and Z_y are analogous to standard deviation and are referred to as moments, hence the name Pearson Product-Moment Correlation. The reader should note that a moment is a measure of variability like the standard deviation.

The r effect size, also called the Pearson correlation coefficient, is biased when applied to independent samples. Essentially, the effect size r tends to be sample specific and biased with small sample sizes and small population effect sizes. Wang and Thompson (2007) recommended the Ezekiel and Smith r squared corrections for controlling such bias. Readers should remember that such corrections are effect sizes. If r squared equaled .01 with a sample size of 10, the Ezekiel and Smith Pearson r^2 corrections are the following:

Ezekiel $1 - [(n - 1) / (n - p - 1)] [1 - R^2]$
             $1 - [(10 - 1) / (10 - 1 - 1)] [1 - 0.01]$
             $1 - [9 / 8] [0.99]$
             $1 - [1.12] [0.99]$
             $1 - 1.11$
             $= -0.11$

Smith $1 - [n / (n - p)] (1 - R^2)$
             $1 - [10 / (10 - 1)] (1 - 0.01)$
             $1 - [10 / 9] (0.99)$
             $1 - [1.11] (0.99)$
             $1 - 1.1$
             $= -0.10$

R^2 equals the Pearson r squared
p equals the number of predictors

A practical example will help clarify the effect size r. Let us suppose that four students were measured on two test anxiety scales denoted by X and Y. Even though four pairs would not permit any real conclusion, this example will help to clarify the r effect size:

	Test Anxiety Scales	
Students	X	Y
1.	58	79
2.	57	76
3.	55	70
4.	54	67

The following are the SPSS and SAS commands for calculating the effect size r:

SPSS   **SAS**
Title "Pearson r".   data pearson;
Data List/X 1-2 Y 4-5.   input x y @@;
Begin Data .   lines;
58 79   58 79 57 76

```
57   76                55  70  54  67
55   70                Proc corr;
54   67
proc print;
End Data.
List .
Correlations Variables =
X Y/
Print = twotail/
Statistics = all/.
```

COUNTERNULL VALUE OF AN EFFECT

Rosenthal, Rosnow, and Rubin (2000) presented a correlational approach to contrasts and effect sizes for the behavioral sciences, and they have introduced a new term called counternull value. The **counternull value** is the nonnull magnitude of effect that is endorsed by the same amount of support as the null value of effect. Stated somewhat differently, if the counternull value were assumed to be the null hypothesis, the resulting probability value would be the same as the obtained probability value for the null hypothesis. Moreover, conceptually, the counternull hypothesis is related to confidence intervals. For example, when a researcher calculates an effect size, the calculated effect size estimate falls between the null value of effect and the counternull value. With symmetrical distributions, such as the normal or t, the calculated effect size falls exactly halfway between the null value of the effect size and the counternull value of effect. Verbally, the formula for the counternull value is two times the obtained effect size value. For non-symmetrical distributions, like correlations, percentages or proportions of successes can be transformed to Fisher's z statistics or logarithmically transformed.

META-ANALYSIS

During the twenty-first century, after hearing about meta-analysis, many clinicians and researchers assumed that it would provide the ultimate truth or answer; however, the reader will shortly see that there are a variety of techniques for performing meta-analyses, and there are several schools of thought on how values can be calculated; hence, there are a variety of effect size measures. There is an excellent program called PASS that performs power analysis. Readers who are interested in this program can find more information at the following Website: http://www.ncss.com/pass.html. Later, I will show readers how to use a free power program called G*Power.

Meta-analysis is a quantitative method for synthesizing the literature, and this technique is not new. For example, Cohen (1977) was one of the first researchers to describe meta-analysis and a related technique called power analysis. The reader should note that the r effect size and the d effect size can be added across several studies to provide an overall effect called a meta-analysis.

There are three concepts related to hypothesis testing; they are Type I error, Type II error, and power. **Type I error** is the level of significance chosen by a clinician or researcher to test the significance of a given statistical test. Type I error is the probability of wrongly rejecting the null hypothesis (no treatment effect) or the probability of rejecting the null hypothesis when it is true (Pituch & Stevens, 2016). In effect, with Type I error one is saying that the groups differ, when in fact they do not. **Type II error** is the probability of accepting the null hypothesis when it is false. For example, we are saying the groups do not differ when in fact they do.

The reader should note that Type I and Type II errors are inversely related; that is, as one controls Type I error, Type II error increases, and as one controls Type II error, Type I error increases. Now, power is the probability within statistical or hypothesis testing of rejecting the null hypothesis when it is false; in reality, **power** is the probability of making a correct decision. As Sapp (2006) noted, Type II error and power are related, because power equals one minus Type II errors; therefore, if a clinician or researcher chooses a small alpha level, Type II error increases and power decreases. In fact, it may not be wise to choose an extremely small alpha level such as .01 or .001, since these values tend to reduce statistical power and inflate Type II error. In summary, meta-analysis and its statistics, called effect size measures, allow a clinician or researcher to determine the degree of effect a treatment has within a population, and it determines the degree to which the null hypothesis may be false.

Returning to the notion of the d effect size, Cohen (1977) provided the following rough guidelines of **d = .2** as a small effect size, **d = .5** as a medium effect size, and **d** = **.8** as a large effect size measure; however, one needs to determine the importance of an effect size by consulting the professional literature (Wolf, 1986).

The d effect size can suggest that a treatment is harmful or it may suggest that a control group is outperforming a control group. This can happen when the effect size measure is negative.

Hedges (1982) argued that the d effect size is biased, and he provided a formula to find a weight d. This formula is accurate when both the experimental and control group sample sizes are greater than 10 and the effect size is less than 1.5.

$$\bar{d} = \frac{\Sigma wd}{\Sigma w}$$

d is the unweighted effect size measure, and w is the reciprocal of the estimated variance of d for each study to be aggregated within the meta-analysis.

When the experimental and control groups have approximately equal numbers of participants greater than 10, Hedges (1982) provided the following formula for w:

$$\bar{d} = \frac{\Sigma wd}{\Sigma w}$$

d is the unweighted effect size
N is the combined sample size for the treatment and control groups

Suppose for our example that we calculated an uncorrected or biased d of .8. And the combined sample size for the treatment group and control group was 80. Substituting in the formula for w:

$$w = \frac{2(80)}{8+.8^2} \quad \frac{160}{8.64} = 18.52$$

Now, if we substituted into the $\bar{d}$ formula:

$$\bar{d} = \frac{18.52(.8)}{18.52} \quad \frac{14.816}{18.52} = .80$$

Even though within this example, the $\bar{d}$ and d are almost equal, when several studies are involved d is a weight average of d. Wolf (1986) provides the following d's, W's, and N's for four fictional studies:

Study	N	d	W
1	82	.60	19.6
2	62	-.50	15.0
3	202	.43	49.4
4	22	.75	5.1

The mean of the unweighted or biased d = (.60 + (-.50) + .43 + .75)/4 = .32. Now, the weight d is the following:

$$\bar{d} = \frac{(19.6)(.60) + (15.0)(-.50) + 49.4(.43) + (5.1)(.75)}{19.6 + 1.50 + 49.4 + 5.1} = .39$$

The reader should notice that the unbiased or weighted d of .39 is slightly larger than the unweighted d of .32. This emphasizes the point that when the sample sizes are greater than 10 participants, the two values are close (Green & Hall, 1984).

Rosenthal (1984) described another effect size that he prefers, which is the Pearson product-moment correlation coefficient. One can transform a Cohen's d to an r using the following formula:

$$r = \frac{d}{\sqrt{d^2 + \frac{1}{pq}}}$$

p is the proportion of the participants of the first of the two groups compared, and q (1-p) is the proportion of participants in the second group that is being compared. Rosenthal provided the following rough guidelines for effect size r. For values of r, **.1** is considered a small effect size, **.3** a medium effect size, and **.5** a large effect size. As Sapp (1997) noted, arithmetic operations cannot be performed on r because as the population correlation coefficient gets further and further from zero, the distribution of r becomes skewed. Therefore, Fisher (1928, p. 172) developed a transformation of r called "Z_r" or Z subscript r. The following is the formula for Z_r:

$$Z_r = \frac{1}{2} \log_e \left[\frac{1+r}{1-r}\right]$$

The reader may remember Table 1 Fisher's zs. Suppose we calculated an r value of .6 with an N of eleven. First, r is divided by 2(N-1), which is the estimated bias.

$$\text{estimated bias} = \frac{.6}{2(10)} = \frac{.6}{20} = .03$$

Now, this bias is removed from Z_r, which is .693 for an r of .60; therefore, we correct or subtract .03 from .693 (Z_r). Corrected Z_r = .693 - .03 = .663, which is associated with an r of .580. If we repeat the calculation for the value of r = .580 and Z_r = .693, estimated bias =

$$\frac{.580}{2(11-1)} = \frac{.580}{20} = .029$$

$$.693 - .029 = .664$$

The value Z_r .664 is associated with an r of .580. Notice that the corrected r of .580 differs from the uncorrected r of .60.

Table 1.3
FISHER'S Z TRANSFORMATIONS OF R TO Z

R	z	r	z	r	z	r	Z	r	z
.000	.000	.200	.203	.400	.424	.600	.693	.800	1.099
.005	.005	.205	.208	.405	.430	.605	.701	.805	1.113
.010	.010	.210	.213	.410	.436	.610	.709	.810	1.127
.015	.015	.215	.218	.415	.442	.615	.717	.815	1.142
.020	.020	.220	.224	.420	.448	.620	.725	.820	1.157
.025	.025	.225	.229	.425	.454	.625	.733	.825	1.172
.030	.030	.230	.234	.430	.460	.630	.741	.830	1.188
.035	.035	.235	.239	.435	.466	.635	.750	.835	1.204
.040	.040	.240	.245	.440	.472	.640	.758	.840	1.221
.045	.045	.245	.250	.445	.478	.645	.767	.845	1.238
.050	.050	.250	.255	.450	.485	.650	.775	.850	1.256
.055	.055	.255	.261	.455	.491	.655	.784	.855	1.274
.060	.060	.260	.266	.460	.497	.660	.793	.860	1.293
.065	.065	.265	.271	.465	.504	.665	.802	.865	1.313
.070	.070	.270	.277	.470	.510	.670	.811	.870	1.333

Table 1.3 – *continued*

.075	.075	.275	.282	.475	.517	.675	.820	.875	1.354
.080	.080	.280	.288	.480	.523	.680	.829	.880	1.376
.085	.085	.285	.293	.485	.530	.685	.838	.885	1.398
.090	.090	.290	.299	.490	.536	.690	.848	.890	1.422
.095	.095	.295	.304	.495	.543	.695	.858	.895	1.447
.100	.100	.300	.310	.500	.549	.700	.867	.900	1.472
.105	.105	.305	.315	.505	.556.	.705	.877	.905	1.499
.110	.110	.310	.321	.510	563	.710	.887	.910	1.528
.115	.116	.315	.326	.515	.570	.715	.897	.915	1.557
.120	.121	.320	.332	.520	.576	.720	.908	.920	1.589
.125	.126	.325	.337	.525	.583	.725	.918	.925	1.623
.130	.131	.330	.343	.530	.590	.730	.929	.930	1.658
.135	.136	.335	.348	.535	.597	.735	.940	.935	1.697
.140	.141	.340	.354	.540	.604	.740	.950	.940	1.738
.145	.146	.345	.360	.545	.611	.745	.962	.945	1.783
.150	.151	.350	.365	.550	.618	.750	.973	.950	1.832
.155	.156	.355	.371	.555	.626	.755	.984	.955	1.886
.160	.161	.360	.377	.560	.633	.760	.996	.960	1.946
.165	.167	.365	.383	.565	.640	.765	1.008	.965	2.014
.170	.172	.370	.388	.570	.648	.770	1.020	.970	2.092
.175	.177	.375	.394	.575	.655	.775	1.033	.975	2.185
.180	.182	.380	.400	.580	.662	.780	1.045	.980	2.298
.185	.187	.385	.406	.585	.670	.785	1.058	.985	2.443
.190	.192	.390	.412	.590	.678	.790	1.071	.990	2.647
.195	.198	.395	.418	.595	.685	.795	1.085	.995	2.994

Note: Any z value is defined as ½ log e [(1 + r) / (1-r)].

Before leaving the topic of meta-analysis, There is an example from Rosenthal and Rosnow (1984) to illustrate how a moderate effect size of r can have important practical significance. Rosenthal and Rosnow compared the results of a treatment and a control group. The dependent variable was whether the patients lived or died. Rosenthal and Rosnow presented the following table:

	Treatment Outcome		Total
	Alive	Dead	
Treatment Group	A=66	B=34	100
Control Group	C=34	D=66	100
Total	100	100	200

Because this example involves a frequency or contingency table for dichotomous dependent variable (alive vs. dead), chi square is the correct nonparametric test statistic, and

where E= chi square = $0^2_1/E_1 + 0^2_2/E_2 + 0^2_3/E_3 + 0^2_4/E_4 - N$

R = the row total
C = column total
N = the number of participants

Es are needed for the following cells:

Row 1, Column 1

$$(1,1) = \frac{100\,(100)}{200} = 50$$

Row 1, Column 2

$$(1,2) = \frac{100\,(100)}{200} = 50$$

Row 2, Column 1

$$(2,1) = \frac{100(100)}{200} = 50$$

Row 2, Column 2

$$(2,2) = \frac{100(100)}{200} = 50$$

$$\text{chi square} = \frac{(66)^2}{50} + \frac{(34)^2}{50} + \frac{(34)^2}{50} + \frac{(66)^2}{50} - 200$$

$$= \frac{4356 + 1156 + 1156 + 4356}{50} - 200$$

$$= 20.48$$

Now, Cramer's phi, a Pearson product-moment correlation for dichotomous dependent variables, is the following:

Cramer's phi = [chi square/N(K-1)]$^{1/2}$
K = smaller of rows or columns
N = the number of participants
Cramer's phi = [20.48/200(2-1)]$^{1/2}$
= [.1024]$^{1/2}$
= .32

Alternatively, Glass and Hopkins (1996, p. 133) defined this correlation as:

$$\text{Cramer's phi} = \frac{bc - ad}{[(a+c)(b+d)(a+b)(c+d)]^{1/2}} = -.32$$

Rearranging our table, a, b, d, c would be as follows:

a = 66   b = 34

c = 34   d = 66

Now,

$$\text{Cramer's phi} = \frac{34(34) - 66(66)}{[(100)(100)(100)(100)]^{1/2}} = -.32$$

We referred to the Cramer's phi of .32 as a moderate effect size, and if we square this Cramer's phi, the variance explained is 10.24%. However, survival rate is increased from 34% to 66%; therefore, effect sizes must be interpreted within the substantive research area. For a detailed discussion of meta-analysis and effect size measure, see Rosenthal and Rosnow (1984), Wolf (1986), Rosenthal (1984), and Hunter and Schmidt (1990). Ferguson (2009) criticized this effect size estimate and recommended risk estimates. Risk estimates are commonly used in medical research, and they estimate the difference in risk for a given outcome between two or more groups (Ferguson, 2009). There are three major risk estimates, and these are the following: relative risk (RR), odds ratio (OR), and risk difference (RD). The formula for the relative risk (RR) is the following:

$$RR=[A/(A+B)]/[C(C+D)$$
$$RR=[66/(66+34)]/[34/(34+66)]$$
$$=[66/100]/[34/100]$$
$$.66/.34=1.941$$

An RR of 1.0 indicates no difference between the groups, and an RR of 2.0 would suggest the control group is twice as likely to report a given condition as the treatment group. Specifically, with this example, the control group has about twice as many dead patients as the control group. Essentially, this corresponds to the 34% who died in the treatment group versus the 66% who died in the control group. Ferguson stated that risk estimates, RR and OR, of 2.0 presents practically significant effects for the social sciences. Interestingly, the results of the RR correspond to a practically significant effect size, and this is especially the case when dependent variables are reliable and valid and when randomized clinical trials are employed. Clearly, alive and dead are valid dependent variables. Ferguson stated that risk estimates, RR and OR, of 3.0 is a moderate effect size, and ones 4.0 or higher are large effect sizes. Finally, Cumming suggested using the difference between proportions as a measure of effect size, and to put a confidence interval around this proportion.

CONFIDENCE INTERVALS AROUND THE EFFECT SIZE R

Unfortunately, although not well known by social scientists, the sampling distribution of the population Pearson product-moment correlation is skewed when the value is other than zero, and when the value is zero, it is symmetrical and almost normal; moreover, the degree of skewness of the sampling distribution of the population correlation is also a function of sample size.

For example, when the population correlation coefficient is not zero and the sample size is small, there is greater skewness within the sampling distribution. Since the sampling distribution of the population correlation coefficient is not normally distribution, the statistician R. A. Fisher developed a logarithmic transformation of r. Suppose a researcher found that the items of two hypnotizability scales had a correlation of .30, how would one construct a 95% confidence interval?

First, using Table 1.3, we find the Fisher's z transformation of .30 which is .31. Next, we calculate the standard error which is 1 divided by the square root of the number of cases minus 3. If we assume that the number of cases is 25, the standard error is .21. The 95% confidence interval is the following: .31 plus and minus 1.96(.21), with the lower confidence limit is -.10 and the upper limit .72, but we have to transform the Fisher's z back to regulation r which becomes -.10 for the lower limit and .62 for the upper limit. The 99% confidence interval can be found by substituting 2.58 for 1.96 and following the same steps. The reader should notice that the confidence interval, -.10, .62 contains zero; therefore, the population coefficient does not differ significantly from zero.

Sapp (2015) reported that are over 40 different effect size measures. Effect sizes are important because they allow for meta-analytic thinking, or they provide a quantitative way of summarizing or synthesizing the literature within an area of hypnosis. Cohen (1977) was one of the first researchers to describe effect sizes and a related area called power analysis. Power is the probability of rejecting a false null hypothesis (population means are equal). Even though there are a variety of effect sizes, two are commonly used within meta-analysis, the correlation, which was discussed within the section on confidence intervals around validity, and the d effect size. The Pearson product-moment correlation or Pearson r is familiar to readers, and Rosenthal (1984) defined value of r of .1 as a small effect size, and a value of .3 as a medium effect size, and a value of .5 as a large effect size. Rosenthal is clear that these are rough rules of thumb and effect sizes have to be evaluated within a substantive area. Cohen (1977) defined the d effect size as the difference between two means divided by the standard deviation or some form of variability.

According to Cumming and Finch (2005), confidence intervals around correlations are the same process described within this book in the section on confidence intervals around validity indices; however, confidence intervals around d effect sizes is more complex and require, like coefficient alpha, non-centralized distributions. In addition, readers who are interested in the software for these distributions can consult Bird (2002) and Smithson (2001). Professor Geoff Cummings, at La Trobe University in Australia, has developed software that runs under the program Excel, and it can be downloaded by doing a Google search. Later within this chapter, the control lines for SAS will be presented for calculating confidence intervals around d.

The highest average effect sizes for traditional cognitive-behavioral orientations or therapies are found in Table 1.1. Cognitive-behavioral therapies are eclectic groups of techniques that combine strategies from cognitive and behavioral psychology. Albert Ellis is the grandfather of cognitive-behavioral therapy within the area of clinical psychology, while Aaron T. Beck is a prominent figure within the area of psychiatry. Traditional forms of cognitive-behavioral therapies developed from academic psychology or were embraced by academic psychology. As previously stated, traditional cognitive-behavioral orientations are found in Table 1.4.

Behavioral therapy is the collection of techniques to change behavior. Hypnotherapy is the therapeutic use of hypnosis to change behavior. Moreover, hypnosis parallels guided imagery, biofeedback, and progressive relaxation. In essence, it is a therapeutic relationship between a therapist and client in which the client receives suggestions that have psychophysiological effects. In addition, hypnosis can lead to behavioral changes and there are several styles or approaches to hypnosis. Systematic desensitization is an imagination technique that pairs relaxation and anxiety-evoking stimuli.

Implosive therapy is also an imagination-based procedure that is similar to flooding, but employs psychoanalytic imagery scenes. Behavior modification is the use of behavioral techniques to modify or change behavior. As previously stated, cognitive-behavioral therapy is a blend of cognitive and behavioral psychology, and it states that clients' problems are the results of faulty belief systems. Cognitive therapy is a form of cognitive-therapy that was developed by Aaron Beck, and the goals are to change clients distorted cognitions.

Self-control strategies are techniques that clients implement themselves, such as self-monitoring, self-reinforcement, self-punishment, bibliotherapy, self-hypnosis, and so on. Biofeedback is the use of computers and other technologies to provide clients with feedback about physiological processes, such as body temperature, blood pressure, and heart rate. Covert behavioral therapy is another imagery-based technique that uses aversive stimuli to desensitize clients to anxiety. Flooding is yet another imagination or in vivo, real-life-based procedure that leads to the extinction or unlearning of behavior.

Relaxation therapy is the implementation of progressive relaxation or muscle-tension exercises or guided imagery to produce relaxation. Reinforcement is a technique that leads to an increase in behavior. Finally, modeling is a social learning technique that employs models to model and modify certain behaviors.

Within Table 1.1, the reader should notice that cognitive-behavioral therapy has a d effect size of 1.13, which is a large effect size, and 475 studies supported this statistic. Interestingly, hypnotherapy has a d effect size of 1.82-again a large effect size measure. Likewise, cognitive therapy has a large effect size of 1.00 with 214 studies to support the overall effect. Moreover, implosive therapy has a medium effect size of .68. In contrast, flooding, a technique related to implosive therapy, has a large effect size of 1.12.

Effect sizes of nontraditional cognitive-behavioral orientations are found in Table 1.2. Adlerian therapy, a forerunner of traditional cognitive-behavioral therapies, is an analytical form of psychotherapy. Transactional analysis is a form of cognitive-behavioral therapy that did not develop from academic or traditional behavior therapy. Within this form of psychotherapy, usually there are not references to classical or operant conditioning, but an analysis of clients' ego states, which is a behavioral way of operationally defining Freud's constructs of personality – id, ego, superego; however, transactional analysis refers to these as the child, adult, and parent ego states, respectively. In contrast to Freud's psychoanalysis, transactional analysis is a humanistic-existential form of psychotherapy that stresses clients can choose and change even when experiencing harsh social and environmental forces.

Reality therapy did not develop from academic psychology either, and it has humanistic-existential and behavior modification aspects. Reality therapy teaches clients to take responsibility for their behaviors and actions and to do things in order for change to occur.

Table 1.5 has the highest average effect size measures for nontraditional cognitive-behavioral therapies. Adlerian therapy had a d effect size of .71, which is a medium effect size. Transactional analysis had a d effect size of .67. which is another medium effect size measure. Finally, reality therapy had a d effect size of .75, which rounded, is approximately .80 – indicating a large effect size; however, there are only 21 studies used in calculating this effect size.

Table 1.6 has the 95% confidence intervals for the highest average d effect sizes for the various forms of psychotherapy along with the power values, and these intervals were calculated with software found Smithson (2003), and this table provides more information than Tables 5.1 and 5.2. As previously stated, SAS can also calculate these intervals. For example, clearly short-term dynamic therapy and reality therapy both have lower power values that the other therapies. Stevens defined power values greater than .70 as adequate and values greater than .90 as excellent. Both short-term dynamic therapy and reality therapy have lower power values because of their small sample sizes. Power is not usually an issue with sample sizes of about 100. The readers should also notice that short-term dynamic therapy and reality therapy both have zeros within their confidence intervals that suggest the null hypothesis was not rejected and negative values within these intervals also suggest that both therapies can produce negative effects or harm; however, clearly any form of psychotherapy can produce negative effects, especially treatments with high effect sizes.

In summary, both short-dynamic therapy and reality therapy have confidence intervals that include zero, and confidence intervals around d provide more information than the single point estimate of d.

Cognitive-behavioral therapy had a lower limit of .4677 (about a medium effect size and an upper limit of .6614, again a value reflecting a medium effect size). Hypnotherapy had a lower limit of .8025 (large effect size) and an upper limit of 1.0163 (large effect size).

Dynamic/humanistic therapy, person-centered therapy, and Gestalt therapy all had lower confidence intervals that are within the lower ranges, with dynamic/humanistic therapy with a lower limit of .0648 – which is the lowest of the humanistic therapies.

In terms of cognitive-behavioral therapies with upper limits of values that are .80 or larger, only hypnotherapy, covert-behavioral therapy, modeling, and reality therapy had upper limits with high d effect sizes using confidence intervals.

Clearly, Table 1.6 provides more information than Tables 1.4 and 1.5. The confidence intervals suggest that true population parameters vary from the d effect size point estimates. Most forms of cognitive-behavioral therapies have upper confidence intervals within the medium effect size ranges, and not the larger ranges as suggested by the point estimates of d.

Table 1.4
HIGHEST AVERAGE EFFECT SIZE MEASURES FOR TRADITIONAL
COGNITIVE-BEHAVIORAL ORIENTATIONS

Orientation	Effect size d	Effect size r	Number of studies
Behavioral therapy	1.06	.48	214
Hypnotherapy	1.82	.68	475
Systematic Desensitization	1.05	.47	475
Implosive therapy	.68	.33	475
Behavior modification	.73	.35	475
Cognitive-behavioral therapy	1.13	.50	475
Cognitive therapy	1.00	.46	214
Self-control strategies	1.01	.46	214
Biofeedback	.91	.42	214
Covert-behavioral	1.52	.61	214
Flooding	1.12	.50	214
Relaxation therapy	.90	.42	214
Reinforcement	.97	.45	214
Modeling	1.43	.59	214

Table 1.5
HIGHEST AVERAGE EFFECT SIZE MEASURES FOR NONTRADITIONAL
COGNITIVE-BEHAVIORAL ORIENTATIONS

Orientation	Effect size d	Effect size r	Number of studies
Adlerian	.71	.34	375
Transactional analysis	.67	.33	475
Reality therapy	.75	.35	21

Table 1.6
CONFIDENCE INTERVALS FOR HIGHEST EFFECT SIZES FOR VARIOUS
FORMS OF PSYCHOTHERAPY WITH POWER VALUES

Orientation	Effect size d	Estimated t-values	95% Confidence interval for d	Power values	Number of studies
Short-Term Dynamic Therapy	.71	1.81	-.0451, .7483	.41	26
Psychodynamic	.69	7.52	.2523, .4374	1.00	475
Dynamic Eclectic	.89	9.69	.3505, .5392	1.00	474
Adlerian	.71	6.87	.2502, .4589	1.00	375
Dynamic/Humanistic	.40	2.93	.0648, .3354	.83	214
Person-Centered	.63	6.10	.2111, .4185	1.00	375
Gestalt	.64	6.97	.2274, .4118	1.00	475
Transactional Analysis	.67	7.30	.2424, .4272	1.00	475
Behavioral Therapy	1.06	7.75	.3861, .6723	1.00	214
Hypnotherapy	1.82	19.83	.8025, 1.0163	1.00	475
Systematic Desensitization	1.05	11.44	.4287, .6206	1.00	475
Implosive Therapy	.68	7.41	.2474, .4323	1.00	475
Behavior Modification	.73	7.95	.2717, .4575	1.00	475
Cognitive-Behavioral Therapy	1.13	12.31	.4677, .6614	1.00	475
Cognitive Therapy	1.00	7.31	.3571, .6413	1.00	214
Self-Control	1.01	7.39	.3624, .6469	1.00	214
Biofeedback	.91	6.66	.3140, .5956	1.00	214
Covert-Behavioral	1.52	11.12	.6072, .9116	1.00	214
Flooding	1.12	8.19	.4151, .7034	1.00	214
Relaxation Therapy	.90	6.58	.3087, .5899	1.00	214
Reinforcement	.97	7.09	.3424, .6258	1.00	214
Modeling	1.43	10.46	.5642, .8645	1.00	214
Reality Therapy	.75	1.72	-.0722, .8083	.38	21

d: population effect size for the t-test for independent two groups and $t = (\sqrt{N/2})d$ and $d = 2t/\sqrt{N}$ According to Stevens (2002), power $> .70$ is adequate and $> .90$ is excellent.

USING SAS FOR CALCULATING THE d EFFECT SIZE CONFIDENCE INTERVALS

Calculating confidence intervals for these d effect sizes involves complex distributions called noncentralized distributions (Steiger & Fouladi,1992; 1997). These distributions do not assume that the null hypothesis is true. Kline (2004) stated that the families of central distribution t, F, and chi-square are special cases of noncentralized distributions. The reader should note that central distributions t, F, and chi-square assume that the null hypothesis is true and they are used for null hypothesis significance testing (NHST). In addition, they are used to determine critical values for test statistics.

Kline (2004) stated that the central t distributions are defined by one parameter, the degrees of freedom; however, the non-centralized distributions are defined by two parameters, the degrees of freedom and the noncentrality parameters. Also, non-centralized distributions, unlike their centralized counterparts, are not centered at zero. When the centrality parameter equals zero for a t-test, the resulting distribution is the symmetrical centralized t distribution. Cummings and Finch (2005) noted that as the noncentrality parameter becomes positive, the noncentral t distribution becomes more positively skewed. In contrast, when the noncentrality parameter becomes increasingly negative, the noncentral t distribution becomes negatively skewed. Essentially, non-centralized distributions are not centered at zero and may not be symmetrical.

SAS can easily calculate non-centrality interval estimations through an iterative interval estimation process. Kline (2004) provided the SAS control lines to compute an exact 95% confidence interval for the d effect size for two groups of participants. The following are the control lines:

SAS Control Lines to Compute an Exact 95% Confidence Interval for Effect Size d for Two Groups of Participants

```
data noncentral_ci_for_delta;
/*two-group design*/
/*data*/
t=3.10;
df=58;
n1=30;
n2=30;
/*lower, upper bounds for ncp*/
ncp_lower=tnonct (t, df, .975);
ncp_upper=tnonct (t, df, .025);
/*lower, upper bounds for delta*/
delta_lower=ncp_lower*sqrt ((n1+n2)/(n1*n2));
delta_upper=ncp_upper*sqrt ((n1+n2)/(n1*n2));
output;
run;
proc print;
run;
```

The reader should note that the only changes in the control lines for a 99% confidence interval is (t, df, .995) and (t, df, .005).

Output

Obs	t	df	n1	n2	ncp_lower	ncp_upper	delta_lower	delta_upper
1	3.1	58	30	30	1.04844	5.12684	0.27071	1.32374

The reader should notice that one has to transform d into t. As noted at the bottom of Table 5.3, $t = (\sqrt{N}/2)d$. If we assume that $d = .8$, then $t = 3.10$. In addition, one has to find the degrees of freedom which is $n_1 = 30$ plus $n_2 = 30$ minus 2 or 58. Within the output section, delta_lower is the lower confidence limit – which is .27071, and delta_upper confidence limit – which is 1.32374.

The following are the SAS control lines for completing an exact confidence interval for the effect size d with one group of participants.

SAS Control Lines to Compute an Exact 95% Confidence Interval for Effect Size d for One Group of Participants

```
data noncentral_ci_for_delta;
/*One-group design*/
/*data*/
t = 1.81;
df = 25
n = 26
/*lower, upper bounds for ncp*/
ncp_lower=tnonct (t, df, .975);
ncp_upper=tnonct (t, df, .025);
/*lower, upper bounds for delta*/
delta_lower=ncp_lower/sqrt(df+1);
delta_upper=ncp_upper/sqrt(df+1);
output;
run;
proc print;
run;
```

Note: Inserting (t, df, .995) and (t, df, .005) will provide a 99% confidence interval.

Output

Obs	t	df	n	ncp_lower	ncp_upper	delta_lower	delta_upper
1	1.81	25	26	-0.22946	3.81558	-0.045001	0.74830

The reader should notice that these are the control lines used to obtain the results for short-term dynamic therapy, where t = 1.81 and the number of studies was 26; therefore, the degrees of freedom (df = the number of studies minus 1 or 25). Again, delta lower is the lower limit – which is -0.045001, and delta_upper is the upper limit – which is 0.74830. The reader should verify how the confidence intervals for d were obtained for the other forms of psychotherapy. Finally, readers can consult Chapter 3 for effect sizes for the difference between two group (between group designs) and the corresponding confidence interval.

CHAPTER SUMMARY

The r and d effect sizes along with their confidence intervals are essential for improving psychological research. Many researchers can calculate the r effect size and put confidence intervals around this value, but many researchers are not sure of what confidence intervals mean. In addition, few researchers know how to use the computer software SAS to calculate confidence intervals around the d effect size. Finally, researchers need to report reliability measures for all items employed within research studies, and they should report confidence intervals around these reliability indices. Within the same vein, confidence intervals are needed for validity indices used within research.

PRACTICE PROBLEMS

1. The following are 8 high school students measured on two test anxiety scales.

   X   Y
   51   53
   52   56
   54   54
   55   57
   51   53
   52   56
   54   54
   55   57

   What is the correlational effect size? How much variance is accounted for?

2. The following are 10 middle school students measured on two self-concept scales.

   X   Y
   50   54
   52   51
   58   60
   54   59
   54   56
   50   54
   52   51
   58   60
   54   59
   54   56

   What is the Pearson correlation?

3. The following are 6 college students measure on two forms of self-efficacy. What is the Pearson correlation?

   X   Y
   57 56
   59 56
   56 53
   62 55
   59 56
   55 54
   57 56
   59 56
   56 53
   62 55
   59 56
   55 54

4. An experimental group population mean equals 7.2 and a population standard deviation equals .41 and the sample size equals 30. For the control group, the population mean equals 5.6, the population standard deviation equals .41, and the sample size equals 30. Calculate the d effect size?

5. A sample mean equals 8.5, the population mean equals 9.5, and the population standard deviation equals .453. Calculate the d effect size?

ANSWERS TO PRACTICE PROBLEMS

1. r=.6 and 36% of the variance is accounted for
2. r=.7798
3. r=.5
4. d=7.2=5.6/.41=3.902439
5. d=9.5-8.5/.453=2.2075061

Chapter 2

CONFIDENCE INTERVALS FOR A SINGLE MEAN

Ferguson (2009) and Sapp (2015) defined a confidence interval as an interval among an infinite number of intervals for a parameter such as population mean, population reliability coefficient, population proportion, population correlation coefficient, population difference and so on, in which one minus the alpha level would capture the population parameter a certain percentage of the time. For example, for a population mean, 95% of these intervals would capture the population mean and $5 = \%$ would not. In contrast to point estimates, which describe sample data, confidence intervals describe population characteristics. More specifically, confidence intervals allow researchers to put a lower limit and upper limit around a population parameter. The 95% and 99% are most used intervals, but any interval width can be established. For the 99 % interval, a researcher is assuming that 99% of these intervals capture these population parameters, and 1% would not. Clearly, a 99% interval is wider than a 95% one (Sapp, Obiakor, Scholze, & Gregas, 2007; Thompson, 2002).

Let us take a practical example. Assume that a university tested a random sample of ten students on the SAT, and the population mean was 708. The following are these student's SAT scores:

708
707
710
708
711
707

708
710
707
709

The mean SAT for this sample is 708.5. However, one student received a 711 and three students obtained a 707. Another way to think of a confidence interval is a band range that includes the difference between the population mean and sample mean plus or minus some error. Interestingly, a confidence interval can be used for hypothesis testing. When the null number of zero is not contained within an interval, the null hypothesis is not rejected.

Table 2.1
ONE-SAMPLE STATISTICS

	N	Mean	Std. Deviation	Std. Error Mean
SAT Score	10	708.5000	1.43372	.45338

Table 2.2
ONE-SAMPLE TEST

	Test Value = 708					
					95% Confidence Interval of the Difference	
	T	df	Sig. (2-tailed)	Mean Difference	Lower	Upper
SAT Score	1.103	9	.299	.50000	-.5256	1.5256

The appropriate test statistic for this design is the one-sample t-test, and statistical significance was not obtained because the level of significance or probability value was .299 for the t-test statistic; a value of .05 or lower is needed for statistical significance. The reader should notice that the 95% confidence interval of the difference between the sample mean and population mean has a lower limit of -.5256 and an upper limit of 1.5256. Since zero is included within the interval, a statistical significance difference was not found between the sample mean and the population mean. These upper and lower limits are found by taking the mean difference (sample mean of 708.5-705 =.50) plus and minus the critical value of t which is 2.262 times the standard error which is .45338. The mean difference of .50 plus 1.02554556 equals 1.5256 rounded to four decimal places. In contrast, the mean difference of .50 minus 1.02554556 equals -.5256 rounded to four decimal places. This suggests that the sample mean is representative of the population mean. The confidence interval for the one-sample case t-test equals the mean plus and minus the critical value of t times the standard error of the mean. If the population mean is not known, the sample mean alone is used to find the confidence interval. Again, the critical value of t for nine degrees of freedom is 2.262; therefore, the upper limit for this confidence interval is:

$$708.5 + 2.262(.45338). \quad 2.262(.45338) = 1.02554556.$$
$$708.5 + 1.02554556 = 709.5255456 \quad \text{upper limit}$$
$$708.5 - 1.02554556 = 707.4744544 \quad \text{lower limit}$$

Finally, we are 95% confidence that the mean SAT score of all these students lies between 707.5 to 709.5, and the sample value of 708 is representative of the population mean or parameter. In summary, point estimates such as 708 describes a sample, and confidence intervals tell us what happens in the population and is an estimate of the population parameter. In essence, it provides an estimate of the mean of all the SAT scores (population)(Sapp, 2004a&b). The following is the general formula for a centralized confidence interval: $\bar{X} \pm (t)$ (Standard Error). X bar is the mean, and t is the critical value of t for the desired confidence interval, and the standard error is found by finding the standard deviation divided by the square root of the number of scores.

PROBLEMS

1. How is hypothesis testing done using a confidence interval?
2. What is a confidence interval?
3. What is the standard error of the mean?
4. What is a one-sample case?
5. Which interval is larger: a 95% confidence interval or a 99% confidence interval?
6. What is the 99% interval for the sample given in this chapter?

ANSWERS

1. If zero or the null number is within the interval, statistical significance is not obtained.
2. Confidence intervals allow one to describe what happens within a population; whereas a point estimate describes a sample.
3. The standard error of the mean is the standard deviation of a sample divided by the square root of the number of scores.
4. A one-sample case is a single sample of data.
5. A 99% confidence interval is larger than a 95% one.
6. 707.03------------709.98

Chapter 3

EFFECT SIZE AND CONFIDENCE INTERVAL FOR DIFFERENCES BETWEEN TWO MEANS (BETWEEN GROUP RESEARCH DESIGNS)

The t-test for independent groups is used for the differences between two group means. This is called a between group design because the two groups are not related in any way. The typical treatment group and control groups is a good representation of this design. If participants are not randomly assigned to groups, there can be threats to internal validity; this means that causal conclusion cannot be made about the treatment. Suppose 15 high school students were randomly assigned to a treatment and a control group to reduced test anxiety, and test anxiety is the dependent variable expressed as t-score, or scores than have a population mean of 50 and standard deviation of 10. Schematically,

Assignment	Group	Dependent Variable
R	Treatment	O
R	Control	O

The R means that this is a randomized design, and the O represents the dependent variable, test anxiety. Suppose the following imaginary data for each group.

Treatment	Control
56	56
58	55
56	56
57	55
59	57

58	55
59	54
56	56
57	57
55	58
59	54
58	55
56	54
58	56
56	57

In this case, we will operationally define the d effect size is the differences between means divided by the average of the standard deviations.

The d effect size is 1.1998, or a large effect size. The SPSS control lines for this design are the following:

> T-Test Groups=GroupID(1 2)
> /Variables=Dependent
> /Criteria=CI(.95).

The means and standard deviations for each group are the following:

	GroupID	N	Mean	Std. Deviation	Std. Error Mean
Dependent	Treatment	15	57.2000	1.32017	.34087
	Control	15	55.6667	1.23443	.31873

The confidence interval for the equality of means were the following:

> The mean difference was 1.533, and the 95% confidence interval for the difference was .57741 for the lower limit and 2.48926 for the upper limit. Because zero is not within this interval, the group means differ at the .05 level of statistical significance.

The confidence interval around d involves the noncentralized t distribution.

Non-centralized distributions are used when the null hypothesis is false, and they are important for power analysis and confidence intervals around d effect sizes. Geoff Cumming's (2012) book *The New Statistics* has a program that runs through Excel, and it is called ESCI (Exploratory Software For Confidence Intervals). The following Figure 3.1 is the print out for the current example.

4 Original units statistics					
		Group 1		Group 2	
	n_1	15		15	n_2
	Mean	57.2		55.667	
	SD	1.3202		1.2344	
	CI ±	0.7311	±	0.6836	0.5
5 Difference (original units)					
	M diff.	1.5333		t	3.286
	SE(diff)	0.4667		p_2	0.0027
Centralized Confidence Interval					
diff)		1.5333	±	0.9559	
				df	28
6 Standardized statistic					
	d	1.1998			
7 ☑ Display CI Confidence interval for δ			☑ Mark ends of CI		
				Lower	Upper
		CI for δ	[	0.0867	2.3129

Figure 3.1. Exploratory Software for Confidence Intervals

The non-centralized confidence interval around the d effect size at the 95% confidence interval is .0867 for the lower limit and 2.3129 for the upper limit. The Greek symbol δ is the non-centralized parameter. As readers may remember, parameters represent population data, and this Greek symbol corresponds to the population effect, while Latin d is the sample effect size.

REGRESSION DISCONTINUITY DESIGNS

Regression discontinuity designs are quasi-experimental designs, and this means these designs have some of the features of a true experimental design such as control group or multiple testing. However, these designs do not randomly assign participants to groups, so all threats to internal validity are not controlled. Cook (2008) provided the history of regression discontinuity designs, or as he stated, they are cutoff-based scores designs. If participants are assigned to a treatment group based on a continuous variable, and that continuous variable is used as a covariate in an analysis of covariance analysis or regression analysis, the selection threat to internal validity is controlled and one can make unbiased causal inferences. With these designs, participants are assigned to a treatment or control group based on if they fell above or below a cutoff score before treatment (Cook, 2008).

Many times, the assignment variable is a pre-test, but it does not have to be correlated with the post-test or dependent variable (Rhoads & Dye, 2016). These designs have the most statistical power when the cutoff scored is placed at the mean of the assignment variable. In addition, more than one assignment variable can be used. Sapp (2014) described a two-group experiment where one group received a treatment for test anxiety and another group served as a control group, but it was impossible to randomly assign participants to groups. Participants were pre-tested for test anxiety before treatment, and participants who scored above the mean were in the treatment group and the participants who scored below the mean on test anxiety were in the control group. After treatment, both groups were post-tested. Here, essentially, participants were assigned to groups based on a cutoff score where one group received the treatment and the other served as a control group. Kline (2009) referred to these designs as a special kind of pretest-posttest design in which participants are selected for the treatment group based on a cutoff score and later the treatment group and control group are given a posttest. The two-group designed described in Sapp (2014) could be depicted as follows:

| Pre-test | Assignment Variable | Treatment | Post-test |
| Pre-test | Assignment Variable | Control | Post-test |

These are between group designs, and these analyses are complex graphical depictions involving a form of regression and complex assumptions. Shadish, Cook, and Campbell (2002) provided a detail discussion of these designs. Finally, these designs are classified as quasi-experimental, and fall somewhere between true experimental designs and quasi-experimental.

Chapter 4

ONE GROUP PRE-TEST POST-TEST DESIGN

The one group pre-test post-test involves the observation of one group at two points in time. Each participant serves as his or her control by providing pretest and posttest (score after a treatment). This design is also called a one-group before-after design. Even though this design is common, It suffers from several threats to internal validity such as history, maturation, and pre-test sensitization. This design is diagrammed as: O1 X O2. The O1 is the pre-test and O2 is the posttest, and X is the treatment. Suppose 12 high school students given a pretest before for test anxiety a test and given a post-test for test anxiety. Suppose the following were these data expressed as t-scores:

Pre-test	Post-test
55	59
72	78
28	30
65	68
84	90
15	20
12	09
23	25
32	29
95	95
52	54
18	24

Even though it is possible to obtain a d effect size for this design, the correlation effect size is simpler and conveys that the conclusions are correlational and not causal. Also, a confidence interval can be placed around the t-test statistic. The SPSS control lines for running this example for the correlation effect size is the following:

> CORRELATIONS
> /VARIABLES=pretest postest
> /PRINT=TWOTAIL NOSIG
> /STATISTICS DESCRIPTIVES
> /MISSING=PAIRWISE

The effect size r=.994, p<.001, and this indicates that the t-test for correlated samples was significant, too. For the paired t-test, the 95% confidence interval was -4.53643 to -.46357. Since zero was not within this interval, statistical significance was reached. The SPSS control lines for the correlated t-test are the following:

> T-TEST PAIRS=pretest WITH postest (PAIRED)
> /CRITERIA=CI(.9500)
> /MISSING=ANALYSIS.

T-Test

Paired Samples Correlations

		N	Correlation	Sig.
Pair 1	pretest & postest	12	.994	.000

Paired Samples Test

		Paired Differences							
					95% Confidence Interval of the Difference				
		Mean	Std. Deviation	Std. Error Mean	Lower	Upper	t	df	Sig (2-tailed)
Pair 1	pre-test - post-test	-2.50000	3.20511	.92524	-4.53643	-.46357	.702	11	.021

PROBLEMS

1. The following represent the test anxiety scores of 16 pairs of fraternal twins. Calculate the correlation effect size, and was a statistical significance obtained?

Fraternal Twins	First Twin	Second Twin
	53.25	53.50
	52.75	52.62
	53.62	53.50
	51.87	51.75
	52.50	52.25
	53.50	53.62
	53.87	53.75
	52.12	52.25
	51.50	51.62
	53.75	53.62
	51.12	51.50
	53.87	53.50
	52.62	52.50
	52.37	52.37
	53.25	53.12
	52.87	53.00

ANSWERS

1. The r effect size was .976, and statistical significance was obtained because the p value was .000.

Paired Samples Statistics

		Mean	N	Std.	Std. Error Mean
Pair 1	Twin1	52.8019	16	.85300	.21325
	Twin2	52.7795	16	.77251	.19313

Paired Samples Correlations

		N	Correlation	Sig.
Pair 1	Twin1 & Twin2	16	.976	.000

Paired Samples Test

		Paired Differences					t	df	Sig. (2-tailed)
		Mean	Std. Deviation	Std. Error Mean	95% Confidence Interval of the Difference				
					Lower	Upper			
Pair 1	Twin 1 - Twin 2	.02238	.19471	.04868	-.08138	.12613	.406	15	.652

95% Confidence Interval of the Difference

The 95% confidence around the paired difference was not significant because zero falls within the interval.

Chapter 5

EFFECT SIZE FOR ONE-WAY ANALYSIS OF VARIANCE OR THREE OR MORE GROUP MEANS

The one-way analysis of variance is used to compare two or more group means to determine if they differ greater than one would expect by change alone. In reality, the t-test statistic squared equals the F-statistic and the square root of the F-statistic equals the t-test statistic (Fisher, 1928). Three or more group means cannot be compared using a series of t-tests, because the overall alpha level, or experimenter error, becomes several times larger than the level set by the researcher, such as the .05, .01, or. 001 alpha level. The thing the reader needs to remember is if one conducts several t-tests, the chances of one yielding significance increases with the number of tests conducted. If one has to conduct several t-tests within the same study, the overall alpha level can be controlled by testing each t-test at the alpha level divided by the number of tests. For example, if one were doing three analyses within the same study at the .05 alpha level, each test statistic would be tested at the .02 or .05/3 level. This method of controlling the overall alpha or Type I error rate is called the Bonferroni inequality or test (Lindman, 1991; Stevens, 2007).

The major advantage of ANOVA is that it keeps the risk of a Type I error small, even when several group means are compared. The one-way ANOVA has the same assumptions as the t-test for independent samples which are normality, homogeneity of variance, and independence. The same things happen to the F-test, which is used to calculate ANOVA, as what occurs when the assumptions are violated under the conditions of the t-test for independent samples.

Previously, it was stated that the t-test and F-test are related. Both tests are special cases of correlation or regression. For example,

$$t = r[(N-2)/(1-r^2)^{1/2}] \text{ and } F = \frac{r^2}{\frac{(1-r)^2}{n-2}}$$

The reader may remember that violating the independence assumption is serious, and this assumption includes the notion that the numerator and denominator of the F-test are independent. When one suspects dependence, which is simply correlated observations or dependent variables, perform statistical tests at a more stringent or lower level of significance such as .01, .001, or .0001 levels of significance.

When observations or dependent variables are correlated within groups, but not across groups, use the group mean as the unit of analysis. Using the mean as the unit of analysis will reduce the sample size, but it will not substantially reduce statistical power since the group means are more stable than individual scores. Finally, if one suspects dependence, calculate the intraclass correlation, and if the correlation is high, perform each statistical test at a lower alpha level such as .001.

With the one-way ANOVA, an F-test or ratio is calculated that is similar to the t-test or t ratio. The numerator of the F-test is called the mean square between groups (MSB), which measures the variability among groups, and the denominator is the mean square within (MSW), or the average variability within groups. In summary, the one-way ANOVA measures variability across groups and variability within groups. The formula for the one-way ANOVA or F-test is the following:

$$F\text{-Test} = \frac{MSB}{MSW}$$

The $MSB = \frac{SSB}{K-1}$, where $SSB = \Sigma n_i (\overline{X}_i - \overline{X})^2$. K = the number of groups, and K-1 is the degrees of freedom for the term SSB, which is the sum of squares between or among groups, and it is a form of variance. Each group mean varies from the grand mean.

The symbol $\overline{X}_i$ is the group mean and $\overline{X}$ is the grand mean. SSB is a weighted sum of squares, because each separate sum of squares is multiplied by its corresponding group size, n_i. The symbol Σ (sigma) means the sum of squares for each group is added across groups. The MSW or mean square within equals the sum of squares within (SSW) divided by the number of participants minus the number of groups. The formula for the $MSW = \frac{SSW}{N-K}$, where SSW equals $\Sigma(X-\overline{X})^2 + (X-\overline{X})^2 \cdots (X$

$-\overline{X})^2$. X is a score of a participant of a given group. The SSW measures how much each score deviates from the corresponding group mean, Σ (sigma) means that the squared deviations $(X - \overline{X})^2$ are added across groups. The N equals the number of participants, K is the number of groups, and N-K is the degrees of freedom for the MSW.

Now we will take an example to illustrate how to calculate the one-way ANOVA. Suppose we had three groups of participants assigned randomly to three treatments for study skills training to improve GRE scores. The levels of the independent variables are in column var00001 and are denoted by numerals 1 through 3. In summary, the independent variable levels are in column var00001 and the dependent variable is in column var00002.

	var00001	var00002
1	1.00	530.00
2	1.00	550.00
3	1.00	520.00
4	1.00	540.00
5	1.00	540.00
6	1.00	530.00
7	2.00	560.00
8	2.00	550.00
9	2.00	560.00
10	2.00	540.00
11	2.00	550.00
12	2.00	530.00
13	3.00	550.00
14	3.00	530.00
15	3.00	540.00
16	3.00	550.00
17	3.00	520.00
18	3.00	540.00

SSB = $6(535-540.56)^2 + 6(548.33-540.56)^2 + 6(538.33-540.56)^2$ = 577.5564. Now we need to calculate the mean square between (MSB), which is just simply SSB/(K-1), where K equals the number of groups.

MSB = SSB/(K-1) = 577.5564/2 = 288.7782. The within group variability is calculated by the sum of squares within (SSW). SSW = $(530-535)^2 + (550-535)^2 + (520-535)^2 + (540-535)^2 + (540-535)^2 + (530-535)^2 + (560-548.33)^2 + (550-548.33)^2 + (560-548.33)^2 + (540-548.33)^2 + (550-548.33)^2 + (530-548.33)^2 + (550-538.33)^2 + (530-538.33)^2 + (540-538.33)^2 + (550-538.33)^2 + (520-538.33)^2 + (540-538.33)^2 = 1916.62$

$$F = \frac{MSB}{MSW} = \frac{288.7782}{127.77} = 2.261$$

Just like the t-test, the F-statistics tests the hypothesis that the population means are equal. Using an F table online, or the one in the back of Sapp (2006), the critical value of F with 2, 15 degrees of freedom is 3.68 at the .05 level of significance, and because the absolute value of the test statistic is not greater than the critical value, we fail to reject the null hypothesis and statistical significance is not obtained. The Microsoft Excel probability value for this F-statistic is .163735. The following are the SPSS control lines for this analysis:

> UNIANOVA
> VAR00002 BY VAR00001
>   /METHOD = SSTYPE(3)
>   /INTERCEPT = INCLUDE
>   /PRINT = ETASQ OPOWER
>   /CRITERIA = ALPHA (.05)
>   /DESIGN = VAR00001.

The following are the SPSS results:

DEPENDENT VARIABLE: VAR00002

Source	Type III Sum of Squares	df	Mean Square	F	Sig.	Partial Eta Squared
Corrected Model	577.778[b]	2	288.889	2.261	.139	.232
Intercept	5259605.556	1	5259605.556	41162.130	.000	1.000
VAR00001	577.778	2	288.889	2.261	.139	.232
Error	1916.667	15	127.778			
Total	5262100.000	18				
Corrected Total	2494.444	17				

TESTS OF BETWEEN-SUBJECTS EFFECTS

DEPENDENT VARIABLE: VAR00002

Source	Noncent. Parameter	Observed Power[a]
Corrected Model	4.522	.388
Intercept	41162.130	1.000
VAR00001	4.522	.388
Error		
Total		
Corrected Total		

The reader should notice that the F-statistic is 2.261 and the probability level is .139, within rounding error. Also, one makes the same decision using the probability value obtained from Microsoft Excel. The computer calculations and hand calculations would be the same. The partial eta squared is .232. The only difference between eta squared and partial eta squared for a one ANOVA is N versus (N-K) in the denominator. For example, eta squared equals (K-1) times F/[(K-1)times F plus (N)], and partial eta squared equals (K-1) times F/[(K-1) times F plus (N-K)]. Cohen (1977) noted that eta squared of .01 corresponds to a small effect size, eta squared of .06 is a medium effect size, and .14 is a large effect size. In summary, the eta squared of .211 is a large effect size, but the power value is .348, indicating poor power. These results show why it is important to calculate effects sizes and power values, especially when one has a small sample size.

The SPSS subcommand for the homogeneity test is the following: / statistics homogeneity. The results of the Levene's test of homogeneity of variances are the following:

TEST OF HOMOGENEITY OF VARIANCES

VAR00002

Levene Statistic	df1	df2	Sig.
2.535	2	15	.113

SAS COMMANDS FOR 95% CONFIDENCE INTERVAL FOR ETA SQUARED

The SAS commands for 95% confidence interval around the population eta squared are the following:

```
data noncentral_ci_for_eta_squared;
/* one-way between-subjects design */
/* data */
F=2.005;
df1=2;
df2=15;
/* lower, upper bounds for ncp */
ncp_lower=fnonct(F,df1,df2, .975);
ncp_upper=fnonct(F,df1,df2, .025);
/*lower, upper bounds for rho-squared */
rho_sq_lower=ncp_lower/ (ncp_lower+df1+df2+1);
rho_sq_upper=ncp_upper/ (ncp_upper+df1+df2+1);
output;
run;
proc print;
run;
```

The following are the results of the SAS:

Obs	F	df1	df2	ncp_lower	ncp_upper	rho_sq_lower	rho_sq_upper
1	2.005	2	15	.	15.0927	.	0.45607

The reader should notice that the lower limit has a "period" indicating 0 and the upper limit is .45607; therefore, the null hypothesis is not rejected because 0 is within the interval. To summarize, within this example the eta squared produced a large effect size, but power was poor and the null hypothesis was not rejected for the F-test.

WELCH AND BROWN-FORSYTHE TEST FOR UNEQUAL VARIANCES

The Welch and Brown-Forsythe Test are used when variances are unequal, and these tests are robust to the violation of homogeneity of variances assumptions. Suppose we had the following data:

GPID	Dep
1.00	10.00
1.00	20.00
1.00	56.00
1.00	90.00
1.00	40.00
1.00	58.00
1.00	50.00
1.00	56.00
1.00	40.00
1.00	20.00
1.00	15.00
1.00	15.00
1.00	30.00
1.00	20.00
1.00	20.00
2.00	56.00
2.00	55.00
2.00	56.00
2.00	55.00
2.00	57.00
2.00	55.00
2.00	54.00
2.00	56.00
2.00	57.00
2.00	58.00
2.00	54.00
2.00	55.00
2.00	54.00
2.00	56.00
2.00	57.00

The following are the descriptive statistics for these data. Clearly, the standard deviations and variances are unequal.

Group Statistics

	GPID	N	Mean	Std. Deviation	Std. Error Mean
Dep	1.00	15	36.0000	22.43403	5.79244
	2.00	15	55.6667	1.23443	.31873

These results of the Levene's test statistically shows that variances are statistically significantly differ with a p value of .004.

Independent Samples Test

	Levene's Test for Equality of Variances		t-test for Equality of Means						
								95% Confidence Interval of the Difference	
	F	Sig	t	df	Sig (2-tailed)	Mean Difference	Std. Error Difference	Lower	Higher
Dep Equal variances assumed	32.138	000	-3.390	28	002	-19.66667	5.80120	-31.54989	-7.78344
Equal variances not assumed			-3.390	14.085	004	-19.66667	5.80120	-32.10199	-7.23134

The following are the SPSS control lines for the Brown-Forsythe and Welch test:

```
ONEWAY Dep BY GPID
  /STATISTICS HOMOGENEITY BROWNFORSYTHE WELCH
  /MISSING ANALYSIS.
```

These are the results for this analysis. Notice that both test are significant with a p value of .004.

If one were to run this analysis with the Levene's test for interpretation, the t=3.390. The square root of the F-test for both statistics equals 11.493, so the square root of this value equals 3.39 or the value for the Levene's test for unequal variances. For more complicate situations, it may be necessary to perform post hoc test with unequal variances, and the follow up tests to the Welch or Brown-Forsythe will provide the correct post hoc tests for unequal variances.

Robust Tests of Equality of Means

	Dep			
	Statistic	df1	df2	Sig.
Welch	11.493	1	14.085	.004
Brown-Forsythe	11.493	1	14.085	.004

If one has more than two groups, the Games-Howell post hoc test for variances that are not equal is the following SPSS control lines:

```
ONEWAY Dep BY GPID
  /STATISTICS HOMOGENEITY BROWNFORSYTHE WELCH
  /MISSING ANALYSIS
  /POSTHOC=GH ALPHA(0.05).
```

FACTORIAL DESIGNS

The simplest factorial design is the two-way analysis of variance or ANOVA. The factorial ANOVA answers three questions. First, do the row means differ significantly? This is referred to as the row main effect. Second, do the column means differ significantly, the column main effect. Third, is the profile of cell means in row one significantly nonparallel to that of row two, the interaction effect?

Interaction also occurs when the profile of cell means for row one can be extended in such a way that it crosses with the profile of cell means for row two. If the profile of cell means is parallel, this indicates the lack of an interaction. Simply stated, an interaction is the multiplicative influence of two independent variables on a dependent variable. *The reader should realize that when there is a significant interaction, it is simply used for interpretation and not the simply main effects.* Technically, there are two kinds of interaction – disordinal and ordinal. With a **disordinal interaction**, the profile of cell means cross, and when the lines do not cross, the **interaction is ordinal**. Consider the following cell means:

	A1	A2	A3
B1	11.00	13.00	15.00
B2	12.00	11.00	10.00

If one were to graph these cell means, the results would be two lines that cross or intersect, and this is referred to as a disordinal interaction. The following profile of cell means would indicate an ordinal interaction:

	A1	A2	A3
B1	42	46	48
B2	40	36	32

To summarize, an interaction effect is the joint interaction of two independent variables on a dependent variables or a group of dependent variables. In a sense, an interaction is differences in differences as one moves across levels. Stated somewhat differently, an interaction is the correlation of two independent variables that differ depending on the levels of the independent variables. The interaction with two independent variables is called a first-order interaction; and the interaction of three independent variables is called a second-order interaction.

As previously stated, a 2x2 or 2x3 factorial design is the simplest factorial design. Sapp (1999) described a 2x2 design where participants were randomly assigned to two groups and measured on test anxiety using the Test Anxiety Inventory that has a mean of 50 and a standard deviation of 10. In addition, participants were separated into high and low hypnotic susceptibility. Schematically, this design is the following:

		Treatments (B)		
		1	2	
	High	50,70	30,60	$\bar{x}_{1\cdot} = 52.5$
Hypnotic Susceptibility (A)		$\bar{x} = 60$	$\bar{x} = 45$	row mean
	Low	50,50	60,60	$\bar{x}_{2\cdot} = 55$
		$\bar{x} = 50$	$\bar{x} = 60$	row mean
		$\bar{x}_{\cdot 1} = 55$	$\bar{x}_{\cdot 2} = 52.5$	$\bar{x}_g = 53.75$
		column mean	column mean	grand mean

With the above example, the dot notation indicates a row. For example, $\bar{x}_{1\cdot} = 52.5$ indicates a row mean. The dot notation in the first part of the subscript indicates a column. For example, $\bar{x}_{2\cdot} = 55$ indicates a column mean. Factorial designs are also referred to as I X J designs, where I indicates the rows and J the columns. If one looks at the independent variable treatments and notices that within parentheses is a B, this refers to the main effect B. We will want to test if there is a significant column effect for B or the treatments. The null hypothesis for factor B is that the population column means $\bar{x}_{\cdot 1}$ and $\bar{x}_{\cdot 2}$ are equal. The independent variable hypnotic susceptibility has an A in parentheses, and this refers to the row main effects for factor A or hypnotic susceptibility. The null hypothesis is that the population row means are equal, $\bar{x}_1.$ equals $\bar{x}_2.$ This design is also called a balanced design because there are an equal number of participants per cell. The reader should remember that SPSS can handle a balanced as well as unbalanced design.

The first things we want to calculate are the main effects for factor A and B. The sum of squares for A=SSA=$nJ\Sigma(\bar{x}_i - \bar{x})^2$, where nJ is the number of participants or observations a row is based on, or more specifically n equals the number of scores within a cell and J equals the number of rows. The sum of squares reflects the variability of the rows from the grand mean ($\bar{x}$). The (2.14) SSA = 2(2) [$(52.5-53.75)^2 + (55-53.75)^2$] = 12.50. The mean sum of squares for factor (2.15) A = MSA = SSA/ (I-1) = 12.5/1 = 12.5. The sum of squares for factor (2.16) B = SSB = $nI\Sigma(\bar{x}_{.j} - \bar{x})^2$. Like the SSA, the SSB reflects the variability of the column means from the grand mean, and the nI is the number of observations each column is based on. The SSB=2(2)[$(55-53.75)^2 = (52.5-53.75)^2$ = 12.50. The mean sum of squares of B = MSB = SSB/(J-1) – 12.50/1 = 12.50.

The next thing to calculate is the error term. This error term is the sum of squares for each cell, and then, these are added or pooled across cells. The formula for the error sum of squares (2.17) = SSW = $\Sigma(X - \bar{X}_{ij})^2$. There are four cells. First, let us take the cell for row one and column one, cell (1,1). The sum of squares for cell (1,1) = $(50-60)^2 + (70-60)^2$. The sum of squares for cell row two and column one, or cell (2,1) = $(50-50)^2 + (50-50)^2$. The sum of squares for cell row one and column 2, or cell (1,2) = $(30-45)^2 + (60-45)^2$. The sum of squares for cell row two and column two, or cell (2,2) = $(60-60)^2 + (60-60)^2$. Finally SSW = $(50-60)^2$, variability for cell (1,1) plus $(50-50)^2 + (50-50)^2$, variability for cell (2,1) plus $(30-45)^2 + (60-45)^2$, variability for cell (1,2) plus $(60-60)^2 + (60-60)^2$, the variability for cell (2,2). Adding the sum of squares across cells, SSW = 650. Now, the mean square within (MSW) equals SSW/ (N-IJ): 650/(8-4) = 162.50; this is the average of the cell variances.

Now, we can test the main effects using F-tests. The main effect of factor A equals (6.18) MSA/MSW = 12.5/162.50 = .08. The degrees of freedom for factor A equals I-1 and J-1, or (1,4). With (1,4) degrees of freedom, the critical value of F at the .05 level of significance equals 7.71. Because the absolute value of the test statistic is not greater than the critical value of F, we fail to reject the null hypothesis. The APA journal format for this statistic is F (A) = .08 (1,4) p>.05.

Now, we can test the main effect for factor B. The F (B) equals MSB/

MSW = 12.50/162.50 = .08. The degrees of freedom for factor B equals (J-1) and (N-1J) or (1,4). Again, the critical values of F with these degrees of freedom at the .05 level of significance are 7.71. *The APA Journal* format for factor B or F (B) = .08 (1,4) p>.05. Like with factor A, F(A), this indicates that the null hypothesis was not rejected or the population columns means are equal. To summarize, for both factors A F(A) and B F(B), statistical significance was not obtained. The reader should remember that the symbol p>.05 means the lack of statistical significance at the .05 level of significance, while the symbol p=.05 means statistical significance at the .05 level of significance.

The next term to calculate is the interaction term. The reader should note that when an interaction is significant, the main effects are ignored because the complexity of an interaction explains data better than the separate simple main effects. Another way of describing the main effects of A and B for a cell is a row or column mean minus the grand mean; therefore, a cell interaction is the cell mean minus the row mean minus the column mean plus the grand mean for a cell. The formula for the estimated cell interaction effect equals $O_{ij} = \overline{X}_{ij} - \overline{X}_{i \cdot} - \overline{X}_{\cdot j} + \overline{X}$, where O_{ij} is an estimated cell interaction effect, or the adjusted cell mean, $\overline{X}_{ij}$ is the cell mean, $\overline{X}_{i \cdot}$ is the row mean, $\overline{X}_{\cdot j}$ is the column mean, and $\overline{X}$ is the grand mean. The following are the adjusted cell means.

		Treatments (B)		Row Means
		1	2	
Hypnotic Susceptibility (A)	High (1)	O_{11} = 6.25	O_{12} = -6.25	52.5
	Low (2)	O_{21} = -6.25	O_{22} = 6.25	55
	Column Means	55	52.5	Grand Mean: 53.75

For cell (1,1) the adjust cell mean equals 60-52.5-55+53.7=6.25. Cell (1,2) the adjusted cell mean is 45-52.5-52.5+53.75= -6.25. The cell (2,1) has an adjusted cell mean of 50-55-55+53.75 = -6.25. Finally, the cell (2,2) has an adjusted cell mean of 60-55-52.5+53.75=6.25.

Earlier it was mentioned that graphing the cell means to display an interaction, but Harwell (1998) pointed out that the **adjusted cell means** should be used to graph interactions. Many textbooks recommend the graphing of observed cell means; however, these can lead to the misinterpretation of interaction effects (Harwell, 1998). As Stevens (2007) pointed out, when graphing real data, the observed cell means will be nonparallel even when the interaction F is less than 1. The sum of squares for interaction SSAB equals the cell size (n=2) times the squared sums of the interaction. Symbolically, the (6.20) SSAB = $n\Sigma O_{ij}^2$ = $2[(6.25)^2 + (-6.25)^2 + (-6.25)^2 + (-6.25)^2] = 312.50$. The mean square for the interaction (MSAB) = SSAB/(I-1) (J-1) = 312.50/(2-1) (2-1) = 312.50. The F statistic for the interaction effect F (AB) = MSAB/MSW=312.50/162.50=1.92. The critical value of F with (1,1) degrees of freedom is 161 at the .05 level of significance; therefore, in APA journal form, F(AB) (1,1) = 1.92, p>.05. Again, the null hypothesis was not rejected and there is not a significant interaction effect.

To summarize, there are **seven steps** for conducting a balanced two way ANOVA. Balanced means that there is an equal number of participants per cell. **First,** obtain the mean and variance for each cell. **Second,** calculate the row, column, and grand means. **Third,** calculate the MSW, or the average of the cell variances. **Fourth,** calculate the sum of squares and mean squares for the main effects. **Fifth,** test each main effect for statistical significance. **Sixth,** calculate the sum of squares and mean square for the interaction effect. **Finally,** test the interaction effect for significance. In Chapter 10, moderation is approached within the context of regression.

FIXED EFFECTS, RANDOM EFFECTS, AND MIXED MODEL ANALYSIS OF VARIANCE (ANOVA)

A fixed effects ANOVA is one where one is not interested in generalizing to some population of interest, and the effects are not randomly sampled from some population of interest; thus, the inferences are fixed to a specific sample. A random effects ANOVA is one where the levels are randomly sampled from some population of interest, and the researcher wishes to generalize beyond the factors in a given study. Finally, a mixed model ANOVA is one with a combination of fixed and random effects. The reader will want to consult Hays (1981) for the correct error term to use in each case.

Before providing the SPSS control lines for this analysis, the reader should realize that some researchers report an ANOVA table for data. With the current example, the ANOVA summary table would be the following:

Source	SS	Df	MS	F	p
A	12.50	1	12.5	.08	p>.05
B	12.50	1	12.5	.08	p>.05
AB	312.50	1	312.50	1.92	p>.05
Within	650	4	162.50		
Total	987.5	7			

The reader should notice that the total degrees of freedom is one less than the total number of participants, but the other degrees of freedom are based on formulas that are specific for the calculation.

Below are the SPSS control lines for running this analysis along with selected output.

```
UNIANOVA
   var00003 BY var00001 var00002
   /METHOD = SSTYPE(3)
   /INTERCEPT = INCLUDE
   /CRITERIA = ALPHA(.05)
   /DESIGN = var00001 var00002 var00001*var00002 .
```

Tests of Between-Subjects Effects

Dependent Variable: VAR00003

Source	Type III Sum of Squares	df	Mean Square	F	Sig.
Corrected Model	337.500	3	112.500	.692	.603
Intercept	23112.500	1	23112.500		.000
VAR00001	12.500	1	12.500	.077	.795
VAR00002	12.500	1	12.500	.077	.795
VAR00001 *	312.500	1	312.500	1.923	.238

Tests of Between-Subjects Effects - *continued*

VAR00002					
Error	650.000	4	162.500		
Total	24100.000	8			
Corrected Total	987.500	7			

a R Squared = .342 (Adjusted R Squared = -.152)

DISPROPORTIONAL CELL SIZE OR UNBALANCED FACTORIAL DESIGNS

When the cell sizes for a factorial ANOVA are unequal or unbalanced, which is the same thing, the effects are said to be correlated or confounded. It may not have appeared with the one-way ANOVA, but the sum of squares are divided into two independent sources of variance, which we referred to as between and within variance. If the factorial ANOVA has an equal number of participants in each size, all effects are independent. Stevens (1999) noted that there are three approaches to unbalanced factorial designs:

Method 1: Find the unique contribution of each effect, or as some statistical programs such as SAS refer to as the Type III sums of squares. With SPSS, this is the default option. With this method, we are adjusting each effect for every other effect in the design. **Method One is the regression effect.**

Method 2: This method is called the **experimental approach**, because we estimate the main effects, disregarding the interaction effect. Next, we estimate the interaction effects, adjusting for the main effects.

Method 3: This is called the **hierarchical approach**, because due to previous research and theory, we establish an ordering of effects, and then we adjust each effect for the preceding effects. Within SPSS, this is called the **sequential approach** and is the Type I sum of squares. For example, suppose we had the following order of effects: A, B, A*B, B*C, A*C, A*B*C.

The reader should remember from the SPSS control lines that an asterisk indicates an interaction. With the sequential approach, the main effect A is not adjusted, but the main effect B is adjusted for the A effect. The interaction effect A*B is adjusted for each main effect, and the interaction B*C is adjusted for by the interaction A*B and the separate main effects A and B. Moreover, the interaction A*C is adjusted for the two interactions B*C and A*B and the two main effects.

Finally, the **second order interaction**, which is the terminology used for factorial designs greater than a two-way design, A*B*C is adjusted by the three first order interaction A*C, B*C and A*B along with the two main effects A and B. In summary, when a factorial design is balanced, all three approaches are the same, but when cell sizes are unequal, the effects within such designs are dependent or correlated because they share the same error term; however, a researcher has to determine which method best explains his or her data. With a randomized design, one may choose Method 2. If there is an a priori ordering of effects, perhaps Method 3 is more appropriate. Generally, it is believed that Method 1 should be used, but the method depends on how a researcher wants to interpret his or her data.

Run the following 2-way ANOVA with unequal cell size:

1.00	1.00	50.00
1.00	1.00	70.00
1.00	2.00	30.00
1.00	2.00	60.00
2.00	1.00	50.00
2.00	1.00	50.00
2.00	2.00	60.00
2.00	2.00	60.00
2.00	2.00	100.00

Below are the SPSS control lines:

```
UNIANOVA
   var00003 BY var00001 var00002
   /METHOD = SSTYPE(3)
   /INTERCEPT = INCLUDE
   /CRITERIA = ALPHA(.05)
   /DESIGN = var00001 var00002 var00001*var00002.
```

Below is the selected output:

Tests of Between-Subjects Effects

Dependent Variable: VAR00003

Source	Type III Sum of Squares	df	Mean Square	F	Sig.
Corrected Model	1172.222	3	390.741	1.138	.418
Intercept	28437.879	1	28437.879	82.829	.000
VAR00001	183.333	1	183.333	.534	.498
VAR00002	37.879	1	37.879	.110	.753
VAR00001 * VAR00002	801.515	1	801.515	2.335	.187
Error	1716.667	5	343.333		
Total	34100.000	9			
Corrected Total	2888.889	8			

a R Squared = .406 (Adjusted R Squared = .049)

The reader should notice that whether a 2-way ANOVA has equal or unequal cell sizes, the SPSS control lines are the same. The following are the SPSS control lines for Method 3, the sequential approach. The only difference is the subcommand method=sstype(1)/.

```
UNIANOVA
  var00003 BY var00001 var00002
  /METHOD = SSTYPE(1)
  /INTERCEPT = INCLUDE
  /CRITERIA = ALPHA(.05)
  /DESIGN = var00001 var00002 var00001*var00002 .
```

Below are the SPSS control lines for Method 2:

```
UNIANOVA
  var00003 BY var00001 var00002
  /METHOD = SSTYPE(2)
  /INTERCEPT = INCLUDE
  /CRITERIA - ALPHA(.05)
  /DESIGN = var00001 var00002 var00001*var00002 .
```

THREE-WAY ANALYSIS OF VARIANCE (ANOVA)

The three-way ANOVA has three independent variables, and with this design the overall alpha level can become extremely high because there are eight sources of variance or two to the third power. The sources are as follows: A, B, and C main effects, AB, AC, BC first order interactions, ABC second order interaction, and within cell or error variance. Since there are eight sources of variance, a significant interaction could be the result of chance and must therefore by hypothesized a priori and tested a smaller alpha level like the .016667, which is alpha .05 divided by 3 or the number of first order interactions within a three-way ANOVA.

A three-way ANOVA tests seven hypotheses and the overall alpha equal 1-(1-alpha level) to the k power, where equals the number of tests, and the upper bound on the overall alpha equals .301. With a four-way interaction, there are 15 hypotheses tested and the upper bound on the overall alpha equals .537. Finally, with a five-way interaction, there are 31 hypotheses, and the upper bound on the overall alpha equals .791. In summary, a three-way interaction is the moderation of two-way ANOVAs by a third moderating variable.

1.00	1.00	1.00	52.00
1.00	1.00	1.00	57.00
1.00	1.00	1.00	53.00
1.00	1.00	1.00	52.00
1.00	1.00	1.00	56.00
1.00	1.00	1.00	58.00
1.00	1.00	2.00	61.00
1.00	1.00	2.00	61.00
1.00	1.00	2.00	60.00
1.00	1.00	2.00	55.00
1.00	1.00	2.00	60.00
1.00	1.00	2.00	58.00
2.00	2.00	1.00	55.00
2.00	2.00	1.00	55.00
2.00	2.00	1.00	57.00
2.00	2.00	1.00	60.00

\multicolumn{4}{c}{Table - continued}
2.00	2.00	1.00	65.00
2.00	2.00	1.00	62.00
2.00	2.00	2.00	63.00
2.00	2.00	2.00	60.00
2.00	2.00	2.00	61.00
2.00	2.00	2.00	62.00
2.00	2.00	2.00	64.00
2.00	2.00	2.00	65.00

```
UNIANOVA
  var00004 BY var00001 var00002 var00003
  /METHOD = SSTYPE(3)
  /INTERCEPT = INCLUDE
  /CRITERIA = ALPHA(.05)
  /DESIGN = var00001 var00002 var00003 var00001*var00002
  var00001*var00003
  var00002*var00003 var00001*var00002*var00003 .
```

MULTIPLE COMPARISONS

There are two kinds of comparisons: a priori or planned, and post hoc or posteriori. Both procedures allow a researcher to test difference among means. As the names suggest, a priori or planned comparisons are planned before research is conduced and a posteriori or post hoc procedures are performed once a significant F-test is found. However, with planned comparison a significant F-test is not required, and they are alternatives to null hypothesis testing. With a three-group ANOVA, and the F-test is significant, there are K(K-1)/2 possible comparisons. Specifically, for three groups, there are two pairwise or two group comparisons.

Planned comparison uses something called contrast. A **contrast** is the differences among means given the appropriate algebraic sign (Sapp, 1999; Kirk, 1982, 1995; Keppel, 1983). In other words, a contrast can be expressed as a **linear combination of means** with the appropriate coefficients, such that at least one contrast is not equal to zero, and the coefficients sum to zero. Mathematically, a contrast can be expressed as the following, where C is the contrast:

$C_i = W_1\overline{X}_1 + W_2\overline{X}_2 + \ldots W_K\overline{X}_K = \Sigma W_i\overline{X}_i$, where $W_1\ W_2\ \ldots\ W$ corresponds to the coefficients or the weights, and $\overline{X}$ = the mean for group K.

A pairwise comparison is one where two coefficients of a contrast are opposite integers such as 1 and -1, and all other coefficients equal zero. Again, the reader should remember that a significant F-test is not needed for planned comparisons. Planned comparisons are used for **theory testing**, and **post hoc comparisons** are used to **explore data** and to explore all possible differences among group means. Actually, planned comparisons are more **precise tests** than the global post hoc procedures, and they are **more powerful** from a statistical point of view than post hoc procedures. Finally, planned comparisons must be based on **strong theory** and **empirical support**.

Planned comparisons have the same statistical assumptions as the one-way ANOVA and t-test for independent groups, and the following three assumptions:

1. Comparisons of hypotheses are planned before a study is conducted.
2. The sum of the weights for each comparison equals zero.
3. K-1 independent comparisons are performed.

With equal sample sizes, two comparisons are independent if the sum of the cross product of their corresponding weight sums to zero. When sample sizes are not equal, independent or orthogonality of comparisons can be expressed with the following equation:

$$\frac{W_{11}W_{12}}{N_1} + \frac{W_{12}W_{22}}{N_2} + \ldots \frac{W_{1k}W_{2k}}{N_k} = 0$$

W_{1k} equals a given weight.
N_k equals the sample size for group

Suppose we were interested in using planned comparisons to test the effects of rational emotive behavior therapy hypnosis, rational emotive behavior therapy, and response expectancies in changing irrational beliefs. With this example, it is possible to perform K-1 or 2 independent comparisons. Suppose theory suggested that rational emotive behavior therapy hypnosis would be the most effective followed by rational emotive behavior therapy. The following contrasts can be tested:

Rational Emotive Behavior Therapy Hypnosis	Rational Emotive Behavior Therapy	Response Expectancies
C1 -1	1	0
C2 0	-1	1

C are the corresponding sets of weights. The cross product of the comparisons' weights are not equal to zero, because C_1 vs $C_2 = -1(0)+1(-1)+0(1)=-1$. The two comparisons are not independent, but the procedure for testing independent and dependent comparison is the same.

The two questions that we have of these data are:

1. Is rational emotive behavior therapy hypnosis more effective than rational emotive behavior therapy?

C1 = -1 1

The negative sign means a reduction in irrational beliefs.

2. Is rational emotive behavioral therapy more effective than response expectancies?

C2 = -1 1

Again, the negative sign means a reduction of irrational beliefs. There is a statistical test to determine if a contrast is significantly different from zero. The null hypothesis for contrast is similar to the ones for the t-test and the one-way ANOVA, it is the population contrast equals zero; the alterative hypothesis is population contrast is not equal to zero.

There are two statistical tests for contrast: one that uses a t-test, and another that uses an F-test. The t-test is the following:

$$t = \frac{C}{(MSW \Sigma W_i^2 n_i)^{\frac{1}{2}}}$$

The F-test is the following:

$$F = \frac{C^2 / \Sigma W_i^2 / n_i}{MSW}$$

Effect Size for One-Way Analysis of Variance

When group sizes are equal, the F-test becomes:

$$F = \frac{nc^2/\Sigma W_i^2}{MSW}$$

Suppose our data were the following, where Group 1 is the rational emotive behavior hypnosis group, Group 2 is the rational emotive behavior therapy, and Group 3 is the response expectancy group:

Group 1	Group 2	Group 3
55	66	66
58	68	57
58	55	60
61	62	54
51	61	57
59	62	73
55	73	62
59	69	63

The SPSS control lines for running these contrasts are the following:

```
Oneway VAR00002 BY VAR00001(1,3)
  /contrast=-1 1 0
  /contrast=0 -1 1/ .
```

The following is the selected SPSS output:

ANOVA

VAR00002

	Sum of Squares	df	Mean Square	F	Sig.
Between Groups	228.000	2	114.000	4.385	.026
Within Groups	546.000	21	26.000		
Total	774.000	23			

Contrast Coefficients

Contrast	VAR0001		
	1.00	2.00	3.00
1	-1	1	0
2	0	-1	1

Contrast Tests

	Contrast		Value of Contrast	Std. Error	t
VAR00002	Assumes Equal Variances	1	7.5000	2.54951	2.942
		2	-3.0000	2.54951	-1.177
	Does Not Assume Equal Variances	1	7.5000	2.28348	3.284
		2	-3.0000	2.91548	-1.029

Contrast Tests

	Contrast		df	Sig. (2-tailed)
VAR00002	Assumes Equal Variances	1	21	.008
		2	21	.252
	Does Not Assume Equal Variances	1	11.015	.007
		2	13.937	.321

The reader should notice that the first contrast was significant, because p = .008 and for the second contrast p = .252, which indicates the lack of statistical significance. Because the first contrast was significant, this means that rational emotive behavior therapy hypnosis was more effective in reducing irrational beliefs than the rational emotive behavior therapy group. The zero for a coefficient means that a group is not part of a comparison. Since the probability value for the second contrast was .252, this means that the rational emotive behavior therapy was not more effective in reducing irrational beliefs than the response expectancy group. The reader should also note that if the homogeneity assumption is not tenable, use the results in the section entitled "Does Not Assume Equal Variances."

Let us confirm how the t value of 2.942 was calculated for the first contrast, substituting into the formulas:

$$C_1 = -1(57) + 1(64.5) + 0(61.5) = 7.5$$
$$C_1^2 = 56.25$$

$$F = \frac{8(56.25)/2}{26} = 8.65$$

with degrees of freedom equaling 1 and the number of participants minus the number of groups, or N-K. In summary, the degrees of freedom equals 1, 21. The reader should remember that $t^2 = F$ or $\sqrt{F} = t$. So, $t = \sqrt{F} = 2.94$. The degrees of freedom for t equals the number of participants, minus the number of groups, or N-K. It is up to the reader to confirm Contrast 2.

POST HOC PROCEDURES

Post hoc procedures are **follow-up tests to significant F-tests**, and they determine which pairs of means are statistically different. One can look at these tests from a liberal to a conservative continuum. The **Fisher's LSD** (Least Significant Difference), **Duncan's new multiple range test, Newman-Kuels, Tukey HSD** (Honestly Significant Difference), and the **Scheffe's** are the common post hoc procedures. The Fisher's LSD is the most liberal and the Scheffe's test is the most conservative.

Liberal post hoc procedures tend to increase the probability that a researcher will find statistical significance when two means are close together, and **conservative procedures** tend to indicate significance when two means are relatively far apart. In summary, **liberal post hoc tests** are **more powerful** than conservative ones, but **conservative tests** like the Scheffe's **control type I error** rate better than liberal procedures. The **Dunnett's test** is another post hoc procedure that can only be used when one has a control group and desires to compare each treatment group with a control group. The Dunnett's can be expressed as the following:

$$t = \frac{\overline{X}_1 - \overline{X}_2}{\sqrt{MSW\left[\frac{1}{n} + \frac{1}{n}\right]}}$$

DF = N-K or the total sample size minus the number of groups.

Post hoc techniques are modifications of the independent t-test. There is little agreement on which techniques are the most appropriate. The Tukey's HSD controls type I errors and provides maximal power. The following is the formula for the Tukey procedure:

$$HSD = Q\sqrt{\frac{MSW}{H_n}}$$

Q = the value of the studentized range statistic that is found by using the within group degrees of freedom and the number of groups denoted by K. H_n is the harmonic mean.

Studentized range statistic is the difference between the largest and smallest treatment means, also called the range, divided by the square root of the mean square error divided by the common group size. Tables for the studentized range statistic can be found in Sapp (2006).

When there are unequal group sizes, the harmonic mean is used and the **Tukey-Kramer** becomes the name of this procedure. The reader should remember that the **harmonic mean** is simply the number of groups divided by the reciprocal of the number of participants. The following is the formula for the simultaneous confidence interval of the Tukey-Kramer procedure:

$$\overline{X}_i - \overline{X}_j \pm Q\sqrt{\frac{MSW}{H_n}}$$

Like all confidence intervals, if the interval contains zero, we fail to reject the null hypothesis and assume that the population means are equal. These are the SPSS control lines for a one-way ANOVA and the Tukey procedure:

```
Oneway
VAR00002 BY VAR00001(1,3)/
ranges=tukey/
harmonic=all/
statistics=all/.
```

NESTED ANOVA

Sapp (2006) stated that **nested designs** are incomplete designs. In other words, these designs are completely crossed, and participants are not in each cell. A completely nested design is one where one level of one factor is paired with one level of another factor. Sapp (2016) described a nested design in which students' test anxiety depended on their schools and teachers. He described a study with three schools and two teachers within each school. Three students were randomly assigned to teachers' classes during an exam. He treated the schools as levels of Factor A and the teachers as levels of Factor B. This resulted in a 6 x 3 design with three test anxiety in each cell. Students are nested with classes and schools. Schematically, this design can be depicted as:

6 X 3 Nested Design			
	A1	A2	A3
B1	70, 68, 64		
B2	69, 70, 70		
B3		64, 68, 64	
B4		62, 62, 59	
B5			63, 66, 63
B6			59, 54, 54

Each level of Factor B is associated or paired with one level of A; in contrast, each level of Factor A is connected with two levels of Factor B.

The SPSS control lines for this design are the following:

Title "Nested Design for Tai Score".
Data list free/Teachers Schools dep.
Begin data.
1 1 70
1 1 68
1 1 64
2 1 69
2 1 70
2 1 70
3 2 64
3 2 68
3 2 64
4 2 62
4 2 62
4 2 59
5 3 63

5 3 66
5 3 63
6 3 59
6 3 54
6 3 54
End data.
Manova dep by Teachers(1,6) Schools(1,3)/
    Design=Schools, Teachers, Teachers
    within schools.

The following is selected output from this analysis:

Tests of Significance for DEP Using UNIQUE Sums of Squares

Source of Variation	SS	DF	MS	F	Sig of F
WITHIN+RESIDUAL	58.67	12	4.89		
SCHOOLS	29.50	2	14.75	3.02	.087*
TEACHERS	140.50	3	46.83	9.58	.002**
TEACHERS WITHIN SCHOOLS	.00	0	.	.	.
OLS					

*This indicates that there is not a significant school effect.
**There are significant teachers nested within schools effect.

Run the following 8 X 2 nested ANOVA on SPSS from Keppel (1991, p. 504).

Title "Nested Design for Tai Score".
Data list free/Teachers Schools dep.
Begin data.
1 1 3
1 1 2
2 1 1
2 1 1
3 1 5
3 1 3
4 1 5
4 1 9
5 2 10
5 2 10
6 2 3

```
6 2 3
7 2 6
7 2 6
8 2 4
8 2 3
End data.
Manova dep by Teachers(1,8) Schools(1,2)/
Design=Schools,Teachers, Teachers within schools.
```

The following are the results of this analysis:

Tests of Significance for DEP using UNIQUE sums of squares

Source of Variation	SS	DF	MS	F	Sig. of F
WITHIN+RESIDUAL	11.00	8	1.38		
SCHOOLS	4.32	1	4.32	3.14	.114*
TEACHERS	100.75	6	16.79	12.21	.001**
TEACHERS WITHIN SCHOOLS	.00	0	.	.	.
OLS					

*The school effects were not significant.
**Teachers nested within schools was significant.

The notion of effect sizes does not make sense for nested designs, and this is due to the clustering of effects that would occur through nested designs. If would were to attempt to find an effect size for a nested design, the result would be ambiguous. To summarize, I presented two nested designs. The term "nested" suggests that dependent variables will not be in every cell; therefore, these are incomplete designs. With each design, Factor B was nested with Factor A. The SPSS subcommand for nested factors is Design=Schools, Teachers, Teachers Within Schools. The "within" part of the subcommand means that teachers are nested within schools. Within experimental design book, the notations B(A) and B/A means that Factor B is nested within Factor A.

The following are the GLM codes for this design.

```
Title "Nested Design for Tai Score".
Data list free/Teachers Schools dep.
Begin data.
```

```
1 1 3
1 1 2
2 1 1
2 1 1
3 1 5
3 1 3
4 1 5
4 1 9
5 2 10
5 2 10
6 2 3
6 2 3
7 2 6
7 2 6
8 2 4
8 2 3
End data.
GLM
Dep by Teachers Schools
  /Method=SSTYPE(3)
  /Criteria=Alpha(.05)
  /Design=Teachers within Schools.
```

The following are the results of this analysis.

Source	Type III Sum of Squares	df	Mean Square	F	Sig.
Corrected Model	116.750[a]	7	16.679	12.130	.001
Intercept	342.250	1	342.250	248.909	.000
TEACHERS(SCHOOLS)	116.750	7	16.679	12.130	.001*
Error	11.000	8	1.375		
Total	470.000	16			
Corrected Total	127.750	15			

a. R Squared = .914 (Adjusted R Squared = .839)

The MANOVA and GLM results are slightly different, but both produced statistical significance at the .001 level. The * denotes teachers nested within schools alpha level, and this effect was statistically significant. And Teachers (Schools) denotes nesting.

Cohen also proposed a standard difference type of effect size for multiple groups or multiple means context (ANOVA), and he used the letter f as this effect size, and it is the following formula:

$$f=[(K-1)F/N]^{1/2}$$

Specifically, the effect size for the main effect A is the following: $f=[(r-1)FA/N]^{1/2}$.
And the effect size for the main effect B is the following: $f=[(c-1)FA/N]^{1/2}$.

FA and FB are the F test for the main effects of A and B respectively. The r is for the row number and c is for the column number. The N is the sample size. An f that equals .1 is a small effect size, and an f of .25 is a medium effect size. Finally, an f greater than .4 is a large effect size.

ONE-WAY ANALYSIS OF COVARIANCE (ANCOVA)

Analysis of covariance (ANCOVA) is a common analysis with randomized pretest posttest control group designs and the nonequivalent control group design. Sapp (2016) cautioned against using ANCOVA with the **nonequivalent control group design** because of pretest measure error. Because of the lack of **randomization** randomly assigned participants to groups, this research design suffers from several threats to internal validity such as **selection** the two groups differing on the pretests, and **regression**, where extreme scores regress toward the mean. From a statistical standpoint, this design is often analyzed by a statistical technique called **analysis of covariance (ANCOVA)**, which is a statistical technique that estimates differences on the posttests by taking into account differences on the pretests.

The difficulty with ANCOVA is it does not work (Huitema, 1980) with nonequivalent control groups due to pretest measurement error. ANCOVA assumes that the covariates were measured without error, but they tend to attenuate or restrict the slopes of the regression lines. Second, this design is called nonequivalent because the treatment and control group differ or are unequivalent on the pretest. The combination of pretest measurement error and group non-equivalence biases the results of ANCOVA for non-equivalent control group designs, but

Huitema provided a possible solution. He recommended constructing new pretest or covariate scores based on the reliability of the pretest scores. It is probably prudent to find several estimates of reliability for the pretest scores, such as coefficient alpha and test retest, and if several forms of reliability lead to the same conclusion, the results are probably tenable. Huitema provides the following formula for adjusting covariates:

$$x_{adj} = \overline{X} + r_{xx}(X - \overline{X})$$
x_{adj} = the adjusted pretest value or estimated true score.
$\overline{X}$ = the covariate mean for partcipants in group J.
r_{xx} = the estimated reliability of the covariate.
x = the obtained covariate score for the ith individual in group J.

These x_{adj} scores correct ANCOVA for unreliability or measurement error. Next, ANCOVA is carried out by using the estimated true covariate scores (x_{adj}) in place of the obtained covariate scores. Finally, even though the nonequivalent control group is a popular design for program evaluation, the design is weak and ANCOVA can produce biased results and adjusted pretest or covariates should be used within the analysis.

ANCOVA combines techniques from regression and ANOVA that allow a statistical rather than experimental control of variables. ANCOVA uses pretests or covariates, which are controlled statistically, to adjust for differences on the posttests, dependent variables, or criteria. Since the pretests are correlated with the posttest, pretests can predict posttests. ANCOVA calculates the proportion of the variance on posttests that existed prior to experimentation. This proportion is statistically removed from the final results. Stated somewhat differently, ANCOVA adjusts posttest means based on pretest means, and the adjusted posttest means are compared to see if they differ significantly.

In summary, ANCOVA is a statistical way to control for the **selection threat to internal validity.** However, this control does not eliminate this threat because it only controls for covariances within the experiment; therefore, groups could differ on variables not used in the experiment. Only randomization minimizes the selection threat to internal validity. ANCOVA tends to minimize the threat with covariates and does not control the threat as well as randomization. Just as the t-test for dependent samples is more powerful than the t-test for independent samples, ANCOVA is statistically more powerful than ANOVA. Very similar to ANOVA, ANCOVA as six assumptions; three are the same as ANOVA. The assumptions of ANCOVA are the following:

1. Normality.
2. Homogeneity of variance.
3. Independence.
4. Linearity — linear relationship between covariate and dependent variable.
5. If there is one covariate, there is an assumption of homogeneity of regression
6. slopes, and with two covariates the assumption is parallelism of regression planes.
7. The covariate is measured without error.
8. Limit the number of covariates to the extent that the following inequality holds:

$$\frac{[C + (J - 1)]}{N}$$

< .10 where C is the number of covariates, J is the number of groups, and N is the total sample size.

If the above inequality holds, the adjusted means are likely to be stable, or the results should be more reliable and cross-validate. When the homogeneity of regression slopes is violated, Stevens (2007) recommends the Johnson-Neyman technique.

The reader should be aware that there are two more alternatives to comparing two or more groups with pre-test and post-test data. One is ANOVA on the difference or gain score (pre-test minus post-test or post-test minus pre-test). Sapp (2006) pointed out that gain scores tend to produce items that are not reliable, and as Stevens (2007) stated, when the correlation between the pre-test and post-test scores approach the reliability of the items, the reliability of the difference scores approaches zero. The second alternative is a two-way repeated measures ANOVA, or what is referred to as a one between (one grouping variable) and one within (pre-test minus post-test or post-test minus pre-test) factor ANOVA. A complicated alternative to ANCOVA, is propensity score matching, and this is a form of matching used when random assignment is not possible. Multiple covariates are used through logistic regression to arrive at propensity scores that are used to reduce the selection bias, and probability of these scores determine if a participant fails in a treatment group or control group (Shadish, Cook, & Campbell, 2002).

Huck, Crocker, and Bounds (1974) compared the two alternative analyses and found ANCOVA to be superior. They pointed out the reliability issue with gain scores, and they also noted that the two-way repeated measures ANOVA is designed to test interaction effects and not just main effects. They noted that the interaction F-test for the repeated measures ANOVA equals the F-test that would be obtained from an ANOVA on gain scores. Finally, whenever the regression coefficient or slope is less than one, which is generally the case during practice, ANCOVA is statistically a more powerful analysis. Suppose 21 test-anxious participants who scored above the mean on test anxiety were pre-tested and randomly assigned to a hypnosis group, relaxation therapy group, and placebo control group. The data and the layout of this design is the following:

Hypnosis		Relaxation Therapy		Placebo Control	
Pretest	Posttest	Pretest	Posttest	Pretest	Posttest
53	56	54	58	53	56
51	54	55	59	52	57
53	55	55	57	52	57
51	53	54	59	53	57
52	54	53	58	54	58
51	53	51	55	51	55
54	56	52	57	54	57

The following are the SPSS control lines for running this analysis:

```
Manova
    posttest BY gpid (1,3) WITH pretest/
    analysis=posttest with pretest/
    print=pmeans/
    design/
    analysis=posttest/
    design=pretest,gpid,pretest by gpid/ *
    analysis=pretest/.
```

*The format for this design subcommand is **covariate, grouping variable, covariate by grouping variable.**

The following is the selected output from this analysis:

Tests of Significance for POSTTEST using UNIQUE sums of squares

Source of Variation	SS	DF	MS	F	Sig of F
WITHIN CELLS	10.30	17	.61		
REGRESSION	16.56	1	16.56	27.32	.000*
GPID	16.93	2	8.47	13.97	.000**
(Model)	53.51	3	17.84	29.43	.000
(Total)	63.81	20	3.19		

* This indicates a significant relationship between the covariate and the dependent variables.
**These are the main results of ANCOVA. They show that the adjusted population means are unequal, indicating statistical significance.

Dependent variable – POST-TEST

COVARIATE	B	Beta	Std. Error	t-Value	Sig. of t
PRETEST	.74286	.55650	.142	5.227	.000
COVARIATE	Lower -95%	CL-Upper			
PRETEST	.443	1.043			

Adjusted and Estimated Means

Variable – POST-TEST

CELL	Obs. Mean	Adj. Mean	Est. Mean	Raw Resid.	Std. Resid.
1	54.429	54.888	54.429	.000	.000
2	57.571	57.076	57.571	.000	.000
3	56.714	56.750	56.714	.000	.000

Tests of Significance for POST-TEST Using UNIQUE Sums of Squares

Source of Variation	SS	DF	MS	F	Sig of F
WITHIN+RESIDUAL	9.63	15	.64		
PRETEST	15.67	1	15.67	24.40	.000
GPID	.83	2	.41	.65	.538
PRETEST BY GPID	.67	2	.33	.52	.605***
(Model)	54.17	5	10.83	16.87	.000
(Total)	63.81	20	3.19		

***This is the test of homogeneity of regression slopes. The slopes are not significantly different because the probability level equals .605, which is not less than .05.

Tests of Significance for PRE-TEST Using UNIQUE Sums of Squares

Source of Variation	SS	DF	MS	F	Sig of F
WITHIN CELLS	30.00	18	1.67		
GPID	5.81	2	2.90	1.74	.203****
(Model)	5.81	2	2.90	1.74	.203
(Total)	35.81	20	1.79		

****This indicates that the participants on the three pretests did not differ.

Adjusted and Estimated Means
Variable – PRE-TEST

CELL	Obs. Mean	Adj. Mean	Est. Mean	Raw Resid.	Std Resid.
1	52.143	52.143	52.143	.000	.000
2	53.429	53.429	53.429	.000	.000
3	52.714	52.714	52.714	.000	.000

The following SPSS commands provide a power analysis and effect sizes:

```
UNIANOVA
   posttest BY gpid WITH pretest
   /METHOD = SSTYPE(3)
   /INTERCEPT = INCLUDE
   /EMMEANS = TABLES(OVERALL) WITH(pretest=MEAN)
   /EMMEANS = TABLES(gpid) WITH(pretest=MEAN)
   /PRINT = ETASQ OPOWER PARAMETER HOMOGENEITY
   /CRITERIA = ALPHA(.05)
   /DESIGN = pretest gpid .
```

As I recommended for the one-group pre-test post-test design, eta squared is a preferred effect size for ANCOVA designs, but is possible to get a Cohen's d measure by obtaining the difference between the adjusted means divided by the square root of the MSW. The MSW is taken from the results of a one-way ANOVA. Readers should note that the covariates are not part of MSW (Pituch & Stevens, 2016).

Chapter 6

CORRELATIONS AS EFFECT SIZES

As stated earlier, correlations and regression are effect sizes; however, there are several types for correlations and various forms of regression. All correlations are effect sizes. **Correlations** measure the association between variables. They can be positive and negative and range between -1.00 and +1.00, where 0 would indicate a lack of a relationship. Correlations were also discussed within the sections on effect sizes. Sapp (1997) reported that there are 16 major correlation coefficients. The **Pearson product-moment correlation** is the most common; it is the basis for deriving other correlation coefficients. The Pearson r, another name of the Pearson product-moment correlation, **measures the linear relationship** between two variables like many correlations. The **independent variable** is denoted by X, and the **dependent variable** is denoted by Y. Another name for the X variable is a **predictor** or **covariate**. As the reader remembers from the chapter on research design, correlation does not imply causation. It is methodologically incorrect to talk about causation with correlations.

The Pearson r communicates two pieces of information. **First,** it shows the magnitude of the relationship between two linearly measured variables. The higher the size of the correlation, the greater the magnitude. Again, the maximum magnitude for the Pearson r is ± 1.00. **Second,** the Pearson r gives the **direction** of the relationship. For example, a Pearson r of +1.00 suggests a perfect, positive relationship. In other words, as the X variable increases, the corresponding Y variable also increases. When the Pearson r = -1.00, this indicates a perfect negative relationship. For example, as the X variable increases, the corresponding Y variable decreases. Finally, when the Pearson r equals zero, there is not a relationship between X and Y.

The **Spearman Rank-Order correlation** is the second most used correlation coefficient. While the Pearson r is used when the X and Y variables are at least quasi-intervaled data, the Spearman Rank-Order correlation coefficient is used when the X and Y variables are ranked from highest to lowest or from lowest to highest on each variable. The Spearman Rank-Order correlation coefficient is also called the Spearman "rho." The Spearman rho is interpreted just like the Pearson r, but the Pearson r tends to be statistically more powerful than the Spearman rho. This is due to the fact that the Spearman rho uses ranked data.

The **point biserial correlation coefficient** is the third most common correlation. This correlation is used when one variable is continuous, a variable taking on an infinite number of values, and the other variable is dichotomous or discrete. For example, if we were interested in the relationship between gender and test anxiety in children, the point biserial correlation would be the correct one.

The **biserial correlation coefficient** is the fourth measure of association. It is used when a continuous a variable is forced into a discrete one, and the other variable is continuous. Suppose we were interested in the correlation between hypnotizability and creative imagination. Here, both variables are actually continuous, but suppose we forced hypnotizability scores into high and low hypnotizability. The correlation between the two variables would be the biserial correlation coefficient. Unlike the point biserial correlation, the biserial correlation only estimates the Pearson r. In addition, the biserial cannot be used in regression equations in order to predict Y values, nor can confidence intervals be used with this correlation. When the assumption of normality is violated, the biserial correlation can be larger than 1.00. In summary, the biserial correlation coefficient is less reliable than the Pearson r or point biserial, and it is not recommended because it is not a very reliable statistic.

The **tetrachoric** is a fifth correlation coefficient. It is used when both X and Y variables are actually continuous and are forced into a dichotomy. Just like the biserial correlation coefficient, the tetrachoric correlation coefficient is less reliable than the Pearson r. Therefore, there is little justification for the tetrachoric correlation coefficient, because the phi correlation coefficient can be used instead.

The **Cramer's phi correlation coefficient** is the sixth correlation coefficient. It is used when both X and Y variables are dichotomous. It is appropriate for two by two contingency tables or larger, where the data are observed frequencies and the researcher wants to determine the strength of association between the two variables within a frequency contingency table. Actually, a statistic called **chi square** is used to determine if a significant relationship exists within a two by two or larger table of observed frequencies. For example, suppose the following observed frequency table existed:

Hypnotizability

		High	Low
Test Anxiety	High	18	32
	Low	29	21

The reader should notice the analogy of this 2 by 2 contingency table and the 2 by 2 factor design.

Chi square = $O_1^2/E_1 + O_2^2/E_2 + O_3^2/E_4 + O_4^2/E_4 - N$ where $E = \frac{R(C)}{N}$
R = row total
C = column total
N = sample size or the number of participants
Es are needed for the following cells:

$(1,1) = \frac{50(47)}{100} = 23.5$

$(1,2) = \frac{50(53)}{100} = 26.5$

$(2,1) = \frac{50(47)}{100} = 23.5$

$(2,2) = \frac{50(53)}{100} = 26.5$

Chi square = $18^2/23.5 + 32^2/26.5 + 29^2/23.5 + 21^2/26.5 - 100 = 4.86$
The degrees of freedom = (R-1) (C-1), and the degrees of freedom equals (2-1) (2-1) = 1.

The critical value of chi square is 3.84 at the .05 level of significance. The rule for assuming statistical significance is the same. If the absolute value of chi square (3.86) is greater than the critical value, we reject the null hypothesis, no difference or there is not a significant correlation or interaction and we assume statistical significance, or there is a significant correlation between the two variables or a significant interaction. In APA journal format, these results are chi square $(1) = 3.86$, $p<.05$. The reader should remember that $p<.05$ means statistical significance at the .05 level, and the degree of freedom is in parentheses. If the calculated value of chi square was 3.78(1), $p>.05$ would indicate the lack of statistical significance.

The reader should be aware that there are one-way chi squares for frequency data. The formula is the same and the expected frequencies are the total number of cases distributed across categories based on some theory a researcher is testing. The degrees of freedom for a one-way chi square is the number of categories minus one (C-1). For example, suppose that a random sample of 100 voters were asked if they would vote for or against a school tax bond. These data would look like the following:

	For	Against	N
O	62	38	100
E	50	50	100

$$\text{Chi square} = 62^2/50 + 38^2/50 - 100$$
$$\frac{3844}{50} + \frac{1444}{50} - 100 = 5.76$$

The degrees of freedom equals the number of categories minus 1 or 1. The critical value of chi square is again 3.84 at the .05 probability level; therefore, in APA format, chi square $= (1) = 5.76$, $p<.05$. These results indicate that a significant number of people support the school tax bond. Once chi square is calculated, Cramer's phi can be calculated with the following formula:

$$\text{Cramer's phi} = \sqrt{\frac{\text{Chi square}}{N(K-1)}}$$

K = smaller of the rows or columns
N = the number of participants
For our example where chi square equals 4.86, substituting into the formula:

$$\text{Cramer's phi} = \sqrt{\frac{4.86}{100(1)}} = .2204541$$

Cramer's phi is interpreted as a Pearson r, but the chi square statistic that is used to find the Cramer's phi should be calculated only when the observations are independent. In other words, do not perform chi square with related or dependent observations. Moreover, do not calculate chi square when the degrees of freedom equal one and any expected frequency is less than five, nor should one calculate chi square when the degrees of freedom equal two and any expected frequency is less than three.

The **correlation ratio**, also called **correlation eta**, is used to measure curvilinear or nonlinear relationships. It was mentioned in connection to analysis of variance. Whenever the F-statistic is calculated, but unlike the Pearson r, eta does not have a sign. The following is the formula for eta:

$$\text{eta} = \sqrt{\frac{\text{between sum of squares}}{\text{total sum of squares}}} \qquad \text{eta squared} = \frac{\text{between sum of squares}}{\text{total sum of squares}}$$

There are four steps for computing eta from an F statistic. For example, suppose F = 26.23, with degrees of freedom of (1,30).

Step 1. Multiply the value by the numerator degrees of freedom.

$$26.23(1) = 26.23$$

Step 2. Add the result of Step 2 to the denominator degrees of freedom.

$$26.23 + 30 = 56.23$$

Step 3. Divide the result of Step 1 by the result of Step 2. This is eta squared.

Step 4. Take the square root of Step 3.

$$\text{eta} = \sqrt{.466477} = .6829912$$

The **Kendall Rank Correlation**, also called the Kendall's tau, is used with rank-ordered data like the Spearman rho, but the advantage of tau is that it can be generalized to partial tau correlations. One limitation of rho is it cannot be generalized to partial correlations.

The **Kendall Coefficient of Concordance** expresses the relationship among three or more sets of ranks. It is the non-parametric version of a multiple correlation, or the correlation of at least two sets of rank prediction and a ranked dependent variable (Siegel, 1956).

The **partial correlation** is a statistical way of controlling for the correlation of a predictor and dependent variable with a third variable held constant. In other words, when a third variable affects the relationship between a predictor variable and a dependent or criterion variable, the partial correlation permits one to partial out the third variable or to hold it constant. The partial correlation can be denoted as $r_{12.3}$, which means that variables one and two and correlated with variable three controlled. The formula for the partial correlation is

$$r_{12.3} = \frac{r_{12} - (r_{13} \times r_{23})}{\sqrt{1-r_{13}^2}\sqrt{r_{23}^2}}$$

With the partial correlation coefficient, the effects of a third variable are removed from both the independent and dependent variable.

The **semipartial correlation** is a variant of the partial correlation, and like the partial correlation it is used with multiple regression (the correlation of at least two predictors and one dependent variable). Cramer and Howitt presented the following formula for the semipartial correlation coefficient:

$$r_x(c.y) = \frac{r_{xy} - (r_{xc} \times r_{yc})}{\sqrt{1-r_{xc}^2}}$$

$$r_x(y.c) = \frac{r_{xy} - (r_{xc} \times r_{yc})}{\sqrt{1-r_{yc}^2}}$$

The difference between the semipartial correlation and the partial correlation is that with the semipartial correlation coefficient, the result of a third variable is only removed from the dependent variable, the independent variable is not adjusted; in contrast, with the partial correlation coefficient, the impact of a third variable is removed from both the independent and dependent variables. The notion of the semipartial or part correlation can be denoted as $r_1(2.3)$. This notation means has been partialled out from variable two but not from variable one; therefore, this is the correlation of variable one and variable two once variable three has been held constant from variable two and not variable one.

The **Kappa Coefficient of Agreement** is used with nominally scaled data. In other words, the number of participants or objects is assigned to one of a variety of categories like the ones used with chi square. Siegel and Castellan (1988) provided the calculations of this correlation.

The **Lambda Statistic**, like the Kappa Coefficient of Agreement, is used with nominal or categorical data; however, it measures the asymmetrical association between variables, which is one limitation of the Cramer's phi coefficient. The Lambda statistic measures the association that may exist differently between the row variables and column variables. In other words, the Lambda statistic provides two correlations, one based on rows and another based on columns. Stated somewhat differently, an asymmetrical correlation is one where the correlation between X and Y is not the same as the correlation between Y and X. Cramer's phi is a symmetrical correlation, because the correlation between X and Y equals the correlation of Y and X (Siegel & Castellan, 1988).

The **Gamma Statistic** is used with ordinally scaled data or rank data with many ties, and it is related with Kendall's tau. See Siegel and Castellan (1988) for a thorough discussion of this correlation coefficient.

The **Somer's D Index of Asymmetrical Association** is similar to the Lambda Statistic but is used with ordinal or ranked data. Again, Siegel and Castellan (1988) provided a thorough treatment of this asymmetrical correlation coefficient. Finally, multiple correlations use two or more predictors and is viewed as a multivariate procedure. The reader can consult Chapter 3 for additional information on multiple correlations or multiple regression. Table 6.1 has a summary of the 16 major correlations.

Table 6.1
SUMMARY OF 16 MAJOR CORRELATIONS

Coefficient	Variables	
	X	Y
Pearson Product-Moment	Continuous	Continuous
Point Biserial	Continuous	True dichotomy
Biserial	Continuous	Continuous, but forced into a dichotomy
Tetrachoric	Continuous, but forced into a dichotomy	Continuous, but forced into a dichotomy
Phi	True dichotomy	True dichotomy
Correlation Ratio (eta)	Continuous	Continuous
Spearman Rank Order	Ranks or capable of being ranked	Ranks or capable of being ranked
Kendall's Coefficient of Concordance	Used with three or more sets of ranks	

Coefficient	Variables	
	X	Y
Kendall's Tau	Ranks or capable of being ranked	Ranks or capable of being ranked
Partial Correlation	Continuous	Continuous
Semipartial Correlation	Continuous	Continuous
Kappa Coefficient of Agreement	Used with nominally scaled data	
Lambda Statistic	Asymmetrical measure of association for a row-by-column contingency table for nominally scaled or categorical data.	
Gamma Statistic	Used when there are many ties on ranked data in a row-by-column contingency table.	
Somer's D Index of Asymmetric Association	Similar to the Lambda statistic, but data is ordinal or ranked. Used to find an asymmetrical association between rows and columns in a contingency data with ordinally scaled or ranked data.	
Multiple Correlation employs two or more predictors	Variables X X Y	

The Pearson Product-Moment correlation is the most common correlation, followed by the Spearman rho. Both of these correlations are symmetrical, but there are asymmetrical correlations like the Lambda statistic and Somer's D. Correlations can be based on continuous, dichotomous, and forced dichotomous variables.

The SPSS control for testing the linearity assumption of a correlation are the following:

    GRAPH
      /SCATTERPLOT(BIVAR)=stai WITH tai
      /MISSING=LISTWISE .

These control lines provide a scatter plot for the X and Y variables.

The following are the data and the SPSS control lines for the Pearson Product-Moment correlation and two nonparametric correlations – Kendall's tau and the Spearman rho:

	tai	Stai
1	58.00	79.00
2	57.00	76.00
3	55.00	70.00
4	54.00	67.00

    CORRELATIONS
      /VARIABLES=tai stai
      /PRINT=TWOTAIL NOSIG
      /MISSING=PAIRWISE .
    NONPAR CORR
      /VARIABLES=tai stai
      /PRINT=BOTH TWOTAIL NOSIG
      /MISSING=PAIRWISE .

The following are the results of these control lines:

Correlations

	TAI	STAI
TAI Pearson Correlation	1	1.000**
Sig. (2-tailed)	.	.
N	4	4
STAI Pearson Correlation	1.000**	1
Sig. (2-tailed)	.	.
N	4	4

**Correlation is significant at the 0.01 level

Nonparametric Correlations

			TAI	STAI
Kendall's tau_b	TAI	Correlation Coefficient	1.000	1.000*
		Sig. (2-tailed)	.	.042
		N	4	4
	STAI	Correlation Coefficient	1.000*	1.000
		Sig. (2-tailed)	.042	.
		N	4	4
Spearman's rho	TAI	Correlation Coefficient	1.000	1.000**
		Sig. (2-tailed)	.	.
		N	4	4
	STAI	Correlation Coefficient	1.00**	1.000
		Sig. (2-tailed)	.	.
		N	4	4

*. Correlation is significant at the .05 level (2-tailed)
**. Correlation is significant at the .01 level (2-tailed)

When a significant correlation is found, it is possible to predict y values (y) from known X values, provided the sample is a random representation of a population. In other words, the sample must be randomly drawn from a population. The lack of a random sample selection is one reason correlation and regression analyses tend not to cross-validate or apply to independent random samples.

A regression equation uses X values to predict Y values. The error in prediction is called the unexplained variation or variance and is defined as $\Sigma(Y - Y')^2$, or the sum of the squared errors in prediction. The explained variation is $\Sigma(Y' - \overline{Y})^2$, just as in ANOVA, $\Sigma(Y - \overline{Y})^2$ equals the total variation or variance.

Since the least criterion is set at a minimum, that is, $\Sigma(Y - Y')^2$ is at a minimum, this becomes an important statistical principle (Sapp, 1999). The equations for predicting Y' (called Y prime) are the following:

$Y' = bx + a$
Y' = the predicted Y score or the prediction for the dependent variable.
b = slope of a straight line or the regression coefficient
a = Y-intercept

$b = \dfrac{rS_y}{S_x}$ S_y = standard deviation of Y and S_x = standard deviation of $a = \overline{Y} - b\overline{X}$

The standard error of estimate for predicted values of Y is the following:

$$\sqrt{\dfrac{\Sigma(Y - Y')}{N}}$$

$$r^2 = \dfrac{\text{explained variation}}{\text{total variation}} = \dfrac{\Sigma(Y' - Y)^2}{\Sigma(Y - \overline{Y})^2}$$

Since $r_2 = \sqrt{\dfrac{\text{explained variation}}{\text{total variation}}}$, when simplified, the standard error of estimate becomes $s_y \sqrt{1 - r^2}$.

If both the X variables and Y variables are expressed as Z scores, the predicted value of Y becomes the following:

Zy' (predicted value of Y) = rZ_x
r = the correlation coefficient
Z_x = the Z value of X.

The assumptions of simple regression are the following:

1. Linearity
2. Homoscedasticity of variance
3. Normality
4. Independence of error

Linearity means that there is a linear relationship between the predictor Xs and the dependent variable Ys. Scatter plots or diagrams can allow one to explore this assumption, and if it is violated, other regression techniques such as curvilinear and coefficient eta can be used.

The **homoscedasticity of variance** is similar to the homogeneity assumption discussed with the t-test and F-test. Simply stated, it means that the variances for columns are equal, and the variances for rows are equal. This assumption is also referred to as **constant variance**. If data are sectioned into columns, the variability of Y is the same from column to column, and if data are sectioned into rows, the variability of X will be the same from row to row. Scatter plots from SPSS can be used to assess this assumption, and SPSS has test for unequal variances.

Like the t-test and F-test, simple linear regression is robust to normality assumption, but it is not robust to independence of errors ($e_i = \Sigma(Y - \hat{Y})$). A violation causes problems as it did with the t-test and F-test. The independence of error assumption suggests that residual values $\Sigma (Y - \hat{Y})$ are independent and normally distributed with a mean of zero and constant variance. Stevens (2002) pointed out that the residuals are only independent when the sample size is large relative to the number of predictors, but residuals tend to have different variances.

Suppose we had five participants who were measured on one predictor and one dependent variable or criterion:

X	Y
12	4
11	3
10	2
9	0
8	1

The SPSS control lines for a simple linear regression analysis are the following:

```
REGRESSION
 /MISSING LISTWISE
 /STATISTICS COEFF OUTS R ANOVA
 /CRITERIA=PIN(.05) POUT (.10)
 /NOORIGIN
 /DEPENDENT y
 /METHOD=ENTER x .
```

The following is the output of this analysis:

Model	R	R Square	Adjusted R Square	Standard Error of the Estimate
1	.900[a]	.810	.747	.79582

a. Predictors: (Constant), X

ANOVA[b]

Model		Sum of Squares	Df	Mean Square	F	Sig.
1	Regression	8.100	1	8.100	12.789	.037[a]
	Residual	1.900	3	.633		
	Total	10.000	4			

a. Predictors: (Constant), X
b. Dependent Variable: Y

Coefficients[a]

Model		Unstandardized Coefficients		Standardized Coefficients	t	Sig.
		B	Std. Error	Beta		
1	(Constant)	-7.000	2.542		-2.754	.070
	X	.900	.252	.900	3.576	.037

a. Dependent Variable: Y

From this output, the reader should notice that ANOVA is a special case of regression, and there is a significant relationship between the X variables and Y variables because F=12.789, p=.037. The correlation between X and Y is .900, and the standard error of estimate equals .79582.

The regression equation is $y' = .90 X - 7$. From the printout, the slope or regression coefficient is found under the headings "Unstandardized Coefficients" and "Standardized Coefficients." When there is only one predictor both regression coefficients are the same, but when there is more than one predictor, (X values), the values can differ. Readers should be aware that **regression coefficients** have a variety of names such as **beta weights**, **standardized regression coefficients**, and **regression weights**. These regression coefficients are effect sizes (Ferguson, 2009). Thompson (2004) made the point that it is a misnomer to call such weights standardized, since the weights are constant for a given data set. To be technically more correct, he prefers the term "weights" applied to standardized measures, not standardized weights. The -7 is also found under the heading "Unstandardized Coefficients," and it is the value near the heading (Constant). Finally, when chosen a correlation as an effect size, some thought should go into the process. In summary, correlation and regression are effect sizes.

Chapter 7

EFFECT SIZES FOR TWO OR MORE PREDICTORS AND ONE DEPENDENT VARIABLE

MULTIPLE REGRESSION

Multiple Regression involves using predictors (Xs), also called independent variables, to predict some criterion or dependent variable (the Ys) (Pedhazur, 1997; Cohen, Cohen, West, and Aiken, 2003; Field, 2013; Pituch and Stevens, 2016). Basically, a set of X values is used to predict a dependent variable. For a one predictor case, the equation is the following:

$Y = bX + C$
b = the slope, which can be expressed as $Y_2 - Y_1/X_2 - X_1$
Note: the slope is an effect size.
C = the Y-intercept

The above equation for Y is called a regression equation. The values of X are **fixed** (predictors); the values of Y are subject to vary.

We are interested in finding a line that best fits the relationship between Y and X; hence, this is called the regression of Y on X. The design below represents the regression of Y on X. The following data are taken from Sapp (1999).

SCHEMATIC DESIGN FOR TWO-PREDICTOR CASE

Schematically, the design for the two predictor case is:

X_1	X_2	Y
52	51	58
53	52	57
53	52	58
54	53	55
55	54	54
55	55	55
55	56	53
57	58	55
58	59	53
58	60	52

This is a schematic design for a two-predictor case. The equation for the two-predictor case is the following:

$$Y = b_1 X_1 + b_2 X_2 + C$$

b_1 is the slope of the dependent variable (Y) with predictor X_1, while the second predictor X_2 is held constant. Similarly, b_2 is also the slope of Y, with predictor X_1 held constant.

C = the Y intercept, the Xs are the **predictors**, and Y is the **dependent variable**. For this example, X_1 represents measures of stress, X_2 are measures of worry, and Y is the dependent variable, the TAI.

There are many methods for selecting predictors such as the forward entry or selection, backward elimination, stepwise selection, and forced entry. The **forward entry** enters predictor variables into the regression equation one at a time, and the first predictor to enter the regression equation is the one with the largest correlation with the dependent variable. If this predictor is significant, the predictor with the **largest semipartial** (a variant of a partial correlation or the correlation of several variables with one or more variables held constant), correlation with the criterion is considered. The formula for the partial correlation is:

$$r_{12.3} = \frac{r_{12} - r_{13}r_{23}}{\sqrt{1-r_{13}^2}\sqrt{1-r_{23}^2}}$$

$r_{12.3}$ denotes the correlation between variables 1 and 2, with 3 held constant. The formula for the semipartial correlation which is used with R^2 is:

$$r_{12.3(s)} \text{ or } r_{1(2.3)} = \frac{r_{12} - r_{13}r_{23}}{\sqrt{1-r_{13}^2}}$$

The **semipartial correlation** also known as the **part correlation,** can be denoted as or $r_{1(2.3)}$. This notation states that variable 3 has been partialed out from variable 2 but not from variable 1; hence this is the correlation between variables 1 and 2 once variable 3 has been held constant from variable 2 and not variable 1.

Once a predictor fails to make a significant contribution to predictions, the process is terminated. The difficulty with forward entry is that it does not permit the removal of predictors from a regression equation once they are entered. In contrast, **stepwise regression,** a modification of forward entry, permits predictors to be entered and removed from regression equations at different steps in the process.

The **backward elimination** starts with a regression equation with all the predictors and attempts to eliminate them one at a time, which is the reverse of the forward entry process. Stepwise selection is a variant of the forward entry process, but at each stage, a test is made to determine the usefulness of a predictor. Predictors can be deleted if they lose their usefulness. The reader should realize that stepwise regression and its variants, forward selection and stepwise discriminant analysis, have been attacked (Thompson, 1995). Sapp (2002) recommended factor analyzing regression scores and forcing them into a regression equation. See Sapp (2002, pp. 78–79) for the SPSS control lines for these analyses. The **forced entry method** forces regression predictors into an equation in a specific order. In contrast, the other methods described tend to allow the computer routines to determine the order of entry of predictors into the regression equations. If one wanted to enter variable X1 followed by X2, the SPSS subcommands are: Enter X1/ Enter X2/.

The reader should realize that there is not a perfect way of selecting predictors, but the forced method is preferred. However, even with this method, regression equations must be cross-validated. Stevens (2002) described how to perform cross-validations in both regression analysis and discriminant analysis with SPSS.

There are four steps to **cross-validation regression equations** (Huck, Cormier, & Bounds, 1974, p. 159). *First,* the original group of subjects for whom the predictors and criterion scores are available are randomly split into two groups. *Second,* one of the subgroups is used to derive a regression equation. *Third,* the regression equation is used to predict criterion scores for the group that it was not derived from. *Fourth,* the predicted criterion scores are correlated with actual criterion scores. If there is a significant correlation, this indicates there was not shrinkage in predictive power. When small sample sizes and many predictors are used, the results for regression tend not to cross-validate, or in other words, the results are sample specific. Approximately 15 participants per predictor are needed for reliable regression equations (Stevens, 2002). If the number of predictors equals the sample size, the multiple correlation – the multivariate analog of the Pearson correlation – equals 1, even if none of the predictors correlate with the dependent variable.

The reader should realize that analysis of variance and regression are related and both are general linear models (GLM) and special cases of structural equations (Kline, 2005). Essentially, almost all inferential statistics are special cases of regression. The following shows the analysis of variance table for regression and multiple regression broken down into sums of squares.

ANALYSIS OF VARIANCE TABLE FOR REGRESSION

Source	SS	Df	MS	F
Regression	SS_{reg}	K	SS_{reg}/k	MS_{reg}/MS_{res}
Residual or Error	SS_{res}	n-k-1	$SS_{res}/(n-k-1)$	

MULTIPLE REGRESSION BROKEN DOWN INTO SUMS OF SQUARES

sum of squares about the mean	sum of squares about regression	sum of squares due to regression
$\Sigma(Y - \bar{y})^2$ df=n-1	$\Sigma(Y_i - Y)^2$ df=n-k-1	$\Sigma(Y' - \bar{y})^2$ df=k

The multiple correlation squared (R^2), the dependent variable (Y), and the statistic F, which is from analysis of variance, are all related in the following ways:

$$R^2 = \Sigma(Y' \, \bar{y})^2 / \Sigma(Y' \, \bar{y})^2$$
Y' is the predicted dependent variable.

$$F = \frac{R^2/k}{(1 - R^2)/(n - k - 1)}, \text{ with df} = k \text{ and } (n-k-1)$$

ASSUMPTIONS OF MULTIPLE REGRESSION

Multiple regression has the following four assumptions:

1. Linearity
2. Homoscedasticity of variance
3. Normality
4. Independence of Error

Linearity is the linear relationship between predictors and the dependent variable, and scatter plots can test this assumption. When assumption is violated, curvilinear statistical techniques and coefficient eta, also called the correlation ratio, can be used.

Homoscedasticity of variance, also called constant variance, is a graphic indication that the variances for columns are equal and the variances for rows are equal.

Normality and independence of error are important assumptions of multiple regression, and a violation of these assumptions will affect the results. As was the case for the t-test and F-test, multiple regression is robust to the normality assumption. Finally, as was the case with the univariate statistics, a violation of the independence of error assumption is serious.

SUPPRESSOR VARIABLES IN MULTIPLE REGRESSION

Suppressor variables are independent variables that suppress or obscure the relationship among interdependent variables because they are correlated with other independent variables, but uncorrelated with the dependent variables. Within a regression context, a statistical technique that deal with predicting variables, Pedhazur (1997) described their counterintuitive concept with the following example:

Suppose 3 variables have correlations as follows:

$$r_{12} = .3 \quad r_{13} = .0 \quad r_{23} = .5$$

If variable 1 is the dependent variable, clearly it is not correlated with variable 3; however, variables 2 and 3 have a correlation of .3. Nevertheless, variables 1 and 3 are not correlated; hence, the correlation between these two variables is 0. Now, the semipartial correlation, also called the part correlation, can be denoted as $r_{1(2.3)}$. This notion says that variable 3 has been partialed out from variable 2 but not from variable 1; in other words, this is the correlation between variables 1 and 3 with variable 3 held constant from variable 2 and not variable 1. The semipartial correlation is as follows:

$$r_{1(2.3)} = \frac{.3 - (.0)(.5)}{(1 - .5)^{1/2}} = \frac{.3}{(.5)^{1/2}} + \frac{.3}{.707} = .42$$

The reader should notice that the correlation between variables 1 and 2 increases from .3 to .42 when variable 3 has been partialed out from variable 2 but not from variable 1. In addition, Stevens (2002) provided the following example to illustrate a suppressor variable:

$$r_{yx1} = .60 \quad r_{yx2} = .0 \quad r_{x1x2} = .50$$

Note that y is the dependent variable and x_1 and x_2 are predictors of y or independent variables. The formula for the semipartial correlation is the following:

$$r_{y\,1.2(S)} = \frac{r_{yx1} - r_{yx2}r_{x1x2}}{(1-r_{x1x2})^{1/2}} = .693$$

Again, the reader should notice an increase in predictive power of predictor 1 (x_1) from .60 to .693. It is not uncommon for suppressor variables to have a negative regression coefficient. A regression coefficient is a number that shows how values of an independent variable or predictor variable are connected with values of a dependent variable of criterion. This value is a part of what is called a regression equation. The formula for a regression equation is as follows:

$$y' = a + bx + e$$

where y is the predict dependent variable, x is the independent variable, a is the y intercept, e is the error term, and b is the regression coefficient or slope. In addition, b is an effect size. Ferguson (2009) stated that a b of .2 is a recommended minimum effect size, and a b of .5 is a moderate effect size, and, finally, a b of .8 is a strong effect size. In summary, when several variables are inter-correlated and negative regression coefficients exist, these variables may be suppressor variables.

Lancaster (1999) cited the earliest study of suppressor variables or effects, which occurred during World War II as an attempt to predict pilot success. Researchers used mechanical ability, numerical ability, spatial ability, and verbal ability to predict pilot success. Interestingly, when verbal ability was added to a regression equation, an equation to predict pilot success, the accuracy of the overall model increased; nevertheless, verbal ability had almost a zero correlation with pilot ability; verbal ability was a suppressor variable. Why did verbal ability increase the utility of the overall regression model? First, verbal ability was required to read the instructions and it was needed to take the paper-and-pencil tests. Second, verbal ability removed the measurement artifact variance from the mechanical, numerical, and spatial ability scores (Thompson, 1992).

Finally, Lancaster (1999) provided the following concrete example of suppression and how the squared multiple correlation R^2 increases to 1.0, perfect prediction. Lancaster described a two predictor case

– that is, two predicts x_1 and x_2, and one dependent variable denoted by y. The correlation of y with predictor one (x_1) was -.707106, the correlation of y with the second predictor was $(x2)$ was 0, and the correlation of the two predictors was .-707106. He provided the following formula for finding the beta weight (β):

$\beta = [r_{yx1} - (r_{yx2})(r_{x1x2})]/1 - r_{x1x2}^2$
The β or beta weight for the first predict is the following:
$\beta_1 = [(.707106-(0)(-0.707106)] / 1- (-0.707106)^2$
$= [(.707106-(0)(-0.707106)] / 1-.49999$
$= .707106/.50001$
$=1.41$

The beta weight for the second predict (β_2) is as follows:

$\beta_2 = [r_{yx2} - (r_{yx1})(r_{x1x2})]/1 - r_{x1x2}^2$
$= [0 - (.707106)(-0.707106)] / 1-.49999$
$= [0 - (-.5)] / .5$
$=1.0$
And he provided the formula for the multiple correlated squared (R^2) as the following:
$R^2 = (\beta_1) (r_{yx1}) + (\beta_2) (r_{yx2})$
$R^2 = 1.42 (.707106) + (1.0) (0)$
$= 1.0$ (rounded to one decimal place)

In summary, suppressor variables are not easy to detect, but with regression research, it is important to study the following: zero order correlations are correlations of each X variable with each Y variable; standardized beta weights or coefficients, or beta weights with a common mean and standard deviation, structured coefficients, which are the correlations of a predictor with a dependent variable divided by the multiple regression equation (Sapp, 2002a; Vogt, 1999; Thompson, 1992). Beta weight, both standardized and non-standardized, are effect sizes. In closing, suppressor variables are elusive but important variables within research.

The reader should notice that the semipartial correlation crystallizes the relationship between variables 1 and 2. Within a multiple regression context (two or more predictors for a criterion), simple correlations cannot determine the usefulness of correlations. Even when a researcher conducts a randomized study, it is possible that intervening variables could affect the results. Unlike independent variables, **intervening variables** are theoretical variables that cannot be seen, measured, or manipulated.

Once a clinician or researcher is aware of these variables, it is possible to operationally define them and to turn them into moderating variables. For example, with cognitive-behavioral therapies, learning is an important factor to consider; however, learning is a theoretical construct or intervening variable that can be operationally defined into a moderating variable.

STRUCTURE COEFFICIENTS WITHIN MULTIPLE REGRESSION

Structure coefficients or **structure correlations,** also called **loadings**, are not affected by multicollinearity, the intercorrelation of predictors, like standardized beta weights. The structure coefficients are widely used with several multivariate techniques, such as **discriminant analysis** and **canonical correlation**. By definition, a **structure coefficient**, also called factor loadings, is the correlation of a predictor with a dependent variable divided by the multiple regression correlation (R) for the entire regression equation (Vogt, 1999). Pedhazur (1997) noted that when standardized beta weights have substantive meaning from a regression analysis, structure coefficients greater than or equal to .30 can be treated as meaningful. In summary, structure coefficients, as Pedhazur noted, are zero order (correlation of one x variable and one y variable) divided by a constant, the multiple correlation coefficient. As previously stated, Pedhazur does not believe that structural coefficients aid with interpretation for multiple regression.

INTERACTION EFFECTS WITHIN MULTIPLE REGRESSION

Even when the assumptions of multivariate regression are tenable, and there are not suppressor variables, the predictors can interact, and are analogous to interaction effects within factorial analysis of variance. The reader interested in this topic can consult Cohen, Cohen, West, and Aiken for a thorough discussion of interaction effects within regression and regression diagnostics. Regression diagnostics can help to identify extremes on predictors and discrepancies in regression analysis. Chapter 10 shows how to test interactions effects.

CROSS-VALIDATION FORMULAS WITHIN MULTIPLE REGRESSION

As previously stated, regression equations and analysis tend not to cross-validate, but SPSS provides adjusted R-squared that is supposedly the coefficient of determination, the adjusted R-squared due to shrinkage. Stevens (2002) stated that this adjusted R-squared is of limited utility and tends not to cross-validate. The formula used by SPSS is the Wherry formula. It was developed by a statistician named **Wherry.** The formula is as follows:

$$R^2 = 1 - (n-1)/(n-k-1)(1-R^2)$$

Stevens (2002) recommends calculating the adjusted R^2 using the following formula by statisticians **Herzberg** and **Stein**. This formula estimates the amount of shrinkage expected under cross-validation for multiple regression. The formula is:

$$R_g^2 = 1 - (n-1)/(n-k-1)(n-2)/(n-k-2)(n+1)/m(1-R^2)$$

In each formula, n is the sample size and k is the number of predictors.

	X1	X2	Y
1	52.00	51.00	58.00
2	53.00	52.00	57.00
3	53.00	52.00	58.00
4	54.00	53.00	55.00
5	55.00	54.00	54.00
6	55.00	55.00	55.00
7	55.00	56.00	53.00
8	57.00	58.00	55.00
9	58.00	59.00	53.00
10	58.00	60.00	52.00

Suppose that 10 participants were measured on two predictors (independent variables of hypnotizability X1 and X2) and measured on a standardized hypnotizability measure. The data for this design are the following:

The SPSS control lines for the backward elimination method are as follows:

>   REGRESSION
>   /MISSING LISTWISE
>   /STATISTICS COEFF OUTS R ANOVA
>   /CRITERIA=PIN(.05) POUT (.10)
>   /NOORIGIN
>   /DEPENDENT y
>   /METHOD=BACKWARD x1 x2 .

The following are selected output from this analysis:

Model	Variables Entered	Variables Removed	Method
1	X2, X1[a]		Enter
2		X2	Backward (criterion: Probability of F-to-remove>= .100).

a. All requested variables entered.
b. Dependent Variable: Y

Model Summary

Model	R	R Squared	Adjusted R Squared	Standard Error of the Estimate
1	.854[a]	.729	.651	1.24540
2	.850[b]	.722	.688	1.17792

a. Predictors (Constant), X2, X1
b. Predictors (Constant), X1

ANOVA[c]

Model		Sum of Squares	df	Mean Square	F	Sig.
1	Regression	29.143	2	14.571	9.395	.010[a]
	Residual	10.857	7	1.551		
	Total	40.000	9			
2	Regression	28.900	1	28.900	20.829	.002[b]
	Residual	11.100	8	1.388		
	Total	40.000	9			

a. Predictors: (Constant), X2, X1
b. Predictors: (Constant), X1
c. Dependent Variable: Y

Regression

Variables Entered/Removed[b]

Model	Variables Entered	Variables Removed	Method
1	X2, X1[a]	.	Enter

a. All requested variables entered.
b. Dependent Variable: Y

Model Summary

Model	R	R Squared	Adjusted R Squared	Standard Error of the Estimate
1	.854[a]	.729	.651	1.24540

a. Predictors (Constant), X2, X1

The 95% confidence interval around R squared is .09461 for the lower limit and .90662 for the upper limit. The Steiger and Fouladi (1997) software can be found at: http://www.statpower.net/index.html

ANOVA[b]

Model		Sum of Squares	df	Mean Square	F	Sig.
1	Regression	29.143	2	14.571	9.395	.010[a]
	Residual	10.857	7	1.551		
	Total	40.000	9			

a. Predictors: (Constant), X2, X1
b. Dependent Variable: Y

Coefficients[a]

Model		Unstandardized Coefficients		Standardized Coefficients	t	Sig
		B	Std. Error	Beta		
1	(Constant)		21.755		4.334	.003
	X1		1.083	-.429	-.396	.704
	X2		.722	-.429	-.396	.704

a. Dependent Variable: Y
b.

Note: the effect size for predictor X1 is -.429 for the unstandardized coefficient, it is -.286 for X2, again for the unstandardized coefficient. The standardized effect size for X1 and X2 is the same value -.429.

The regression equation for this analysis is the following:

$$Y' = -.429X1 - .286X2 + 94.286$$

The SPSS control lines for the forced method are the following:

```
REGRESSION
/MISSING LISTWISE
/STATISTICS COEFF OUTS R ANOVA
/CRITERIA=PIN(.05) POUT (.10)
/NOORIGIN
/DEPENDENT y
/METHOD=ENTER x1 x2 .
```

The SPSS control lines for the stepwise procedure are the following:

```
REGRESSION
 /MISSING LISTWISE
 /STATISTICS COEFF OUTS R ANOVA
 /CRITERIA=PIN(.05) POUT (.10)
 /NOORIGIN
 /DEPENDENT y
 /METHOD=STEPWISE x1 x2 .
```

The following are selected output from this analysis.

Coefficients[a]

Model		Unstandardized Coefficients		Standardized Coefficients	t	Sig
		B	Std. Error	Beta		
1	(Constant)	8.571	2.016		4.251	.004
	X1	-.429	1.083	-.429	-.396	.704
	X2	-.286	.722	-.429	-.396	.704

c. Dependent Variable: Y

The regression equation for this analysis is the following:

$$Y' = -.429 - .286 + 8.571$$

The reader should notice that there is a slightly different regression equation than the one obtained from the backward elimination procedure. The reader should also notice that under the column labeled "Beta" from the printout are the beta weights that are analogous to Z-scores because they have a mean of 0 and a standard deviation of 1. The beta weights for each predictor equals -.429. Neither is significant because the p-values are .704 for each predictor.

LOGISTIC REGRESSION

The reader interested in a primer and more detailed discussion of logistic regression can consult Pampel (2000) Menard (2002), Field

(2013) and Pituch and Stevens (2016). As previously stated, multiple regression is a method to analyze the linear relationship between predictors and a dependent variable. Moreover, multiple regression allows a researcher to determine how much variance is accounted for by predictors, or multiple R squared. In addition, multiple regression can be used to determine if two predictors interact, which is analogous to moderator variables.

As previously emphasized, the **forced entry** is also called **hierarchical** or **sequential regression**, because it allows the researcher to determine the order and number of predictors that enter a regression equation. **Logistic regression**, unlike ordinary least squares regression, is appropriate when the dependent variable is dichotomous. The reader may hear the term binomial or binary to describe logistic regression models that have a binary dependent variable, such as zeros and ones. Suppose 10 students were measured on two predictors of test anxiety (X1 and X2) and the dependent variable was passing an examination (one) or failing an examination (zero). The following is this design:

	x1	x2	y
1	52.00	51.00	.00
2	53.00	52.00	.00
3	53.00	52.00	.00
4	54.00	53.00	.00
5	55.00	54.00	.00
6	55.00	55.00	1.00
7	55.00	56.00	1.00
8	57.00	58.00	1.00
9	58.00	59.00	1.00
10	58.00	60.00	1.00

The assumptions of least squares multiple regression or ordinary least squares does not apply to dichotomous or polychotomous dependent variables. A method called **maximum likelihood estimation** is the correct method for such data. This method is used in structural equations modeling and with item response theory, and it tends to maximize the probability that sample statistics are representative of population parameters. In essence, it tends to maximize the probability or likelihood of getting the data one obtained. There are several problems that arise when a dependent variable is dichotomous. First, there are nonnormal error terms. Second, homoscedasticity or variance assumption is violated and there are constraints on the response function (Stevens, 2002). Finally, the relationship between the predictors and dependent variable is an "S" shaped or nonlinear function. The basic ideas that apply to ordinary least squares regression such as method of entry of predictors apply to logistic regression. The following are the SPSS codes for running logistic regression for the example provided:

```
LOGISTIC REGRESSION VAR=y
   /METHOD=ENTER x1 x2
   /CRITERIA PIN(.05) POUT(.10) ITERATE(20) CUT(.5) .
```

The reader should notice from these codes that both predictors were forced into the regression equation. The following are annotated printouts from this analysis:

Variables in the Equation

		B	S.E.	Wald	df	Sig.	Exp(b)
Step 1[a]	X1	-38.275	29467.877	.000	1	.999	.000
	X2	38.281	21066.397	.000	1	.999	4.22E+16
	Constant	17.824	554009.54	.000	1	1.000	55062298

a. Variable(s) entered on step 1: X1, X2

The reader should notice that neither predictor was significantly related to the dependent variable. The following are the SPSS codes for testing the interaction of the two predictors:

```
LOGISTIC REGRESSION VAR=y
   /METHOD=ENTER x1* x2
   /CRITERIA PIN(.05) POUT(.10) ITERATE(20) CUT(.5) .
```

And the following are annotated results from this analysis:

Variables in the Equation

		B	S.E.	Wald	df	Sig.	Exp(b)
Step 1ª	X1 by X2	.591	87.180	.000	1	.995	1.806
	Constant	-1772.054	261394.37	.000	1	.995	.000

a. Variable(s) entered on step 1: X1, X2

The reader should notice from the printout that "Step X1 by X2" tests the interaction of the two predictors, which is analogous to a two-way interaction from analysis of variable. In summary, the two predictors did not interact, or one predictor did not moderate a significant relationship between one predictor and the dependent variable. Finally, the p-value for the interaction effect is .995, indicating a lack of significant interaction.

Chapter 8

EFFECT SIZE FOR TWO OR MORE PREDICTORS AND TWO OR MORE DEPENDENT VARIABLES

MULTIVARIATE REGRESSION

Whereas multiple regression is the relationship between a set of predictors and a dependent variable, multivariate regression is the relationship between a set of predictors and a set of dependent variables, at least two or more. The following example represents 3 dependent variables and two predictors. This design and statistical test allows one to test statistically the relationship between a set of predictors and a set of predictors. And if the is multivariate statistical significance, which variables contribute to the significant.

	tai1	tai2	tai3	x1	x2
1	52.00	51.00	58.00	1.00	.00
2	53.00	52.00	57.00	1.00	.00
3	53.00	52.00	58.00	1.00	.00
4	54.00	53.00	55.00	.00	1.00
5	55.00	54.00	54.00	.00	1.00
6	55.00	55.00	55.00	.00	1.00
7	55.00	56.00	53.00	.00	.00
8	57.00	58.00	55.00	.00	.00
9	58.00	59.00	53.00	.00	.00
10	58.00	60.00	52.00	.00	.00

The reader should notice that the predictors are zero and one, which is called dummy coding of the predictors. A dummy variable is a dichotomous variable that is usually coded by ones and zeros. The participants who are coded as one-zero (1-0) are group one, the ones coded as zero-one (0-1) are in group two, and finally the ones coded as zero-zero (0-0) are in group three. In essence, participants in group one have the following dummy coding: 1 0, ones in group two has the coding 0 1, and finally, group three has the following coding: 0 0. This design is often referred to as a three-group or K group, since there are more than two groups, multivariate analysis of variance (Manova). Manova is the multivariate generalization of analysis of variance (Anova), hence, within this case, participants are measured on three dependent variables, TAI1, TAI2, and TAI 3. Even if participants were only measured on two dependent variables, the design is still multivariate. It should be apparent to the reader that the term multivariate has a variety of definitions. One, with the multiple regression context, participants are measured on two or more predictors and a dependent variable. Second, within a multivariate context participants are measured on two or more predictors and two or more dependent variables. The reader should realize that Manova is a special case of multivariate regression, and as emphasized throughout this book, regression is the cornerstone of most statistical procedures. The following are the SPSS Manova codes for this analysis:

> Manova x1 x2 with tai1 tai2 tai3/
> print=cellinfo(means,cor)/.

The following is annotated output from this analysis. The reader should focus on Wilks' Lambda, which is one of the four multivariate tests that has a p-value of .004, indicating a statistically significant relationship between the predictors and the dependent variables, and this is how one would report this effect size. The univariate f-tests evaluate the significance of the regression of each predictor variable separately. Only X1 is significantly related to the dependent variables, the p-value equals .016. The multiple R squared for X1 equals .80164, and for X2 it is .61330. The p-value equals .106, indicating the lack of statistical significance for this multiple regression analysis.

───────── Analysis of Variance – Design 1 ─────────

EFFECT .. WITHIN CELLS Regression
Multivariate Tests of Significance (S = 2, M = 0, N = 1 ½)

Test Name	Value	Approx. F	Hypoth. DF	Error DF	Sig. of F
Pillai's	1.51193	6.19559	6.00	12.00	.004
Hotelling's	11.60156	7.73437	6.00	8.00	.005
Wilks'	.03588	7.13172	6.00	10.00	.004
Roy's	.90981				

Note.. F statistic for WILKS' Lambda is exact.

EFFECT .. WITHIN CELLS Regression (Cont.)
Univariate F-tests with (3,6) D. F.

Variable	Sq. Mul. R	Adj. R-sq.	Hypoth. MS	Error MS	F
X1	.80164	.70245	.56115	.06943	8.08250
X2	.61330	.41995	.42931	.13535	3.17194

Variable	Sig. of F
X1	.016
X2	.106

The following are the SPSS codes for the general linear model (GLM) for this analysis:

```
GLM
    tai1 tai2 tai3 WITH x1 x2
    /METHOD = SSTYPE(3)
    /INTERCEPT = INCLUDE
    /CRITERIA = ALPHA(.05)
    /DESIGN = x1 x2
```

In summary, this design found a statistically significant relationship between the predictors and dependent variables at the multivariate level, but only predictor X1 was significant at the multiple regression level. Specifically, X1 had a square multiple correlation of .80164, and an adjusted multiple correlation squared of .70245. Both of values are effect sizes or variances account for on the three dependent variables. The adjusted multiple correlation squared is a corrected value, while the other value is an uncorrected effect size. Both effect sizes are squared correlations. Finally, eta squared, the correlation measure of effect, can also be used with MANOVA designs.

Chapter 9

EFFECT SIZE FOR TWO-GROUP MULTIVARIATE ANALYSIS OF VARIANCE

Multivariate analysis of variance (MANOVA) is the multivariate generalization of analysis of variance (ANOVA). The difference between MANOVA and ANOVA is that with MANOVA participants are measured on two or more dependent variables. Because MANOVA combines small difference among dependent variables and it takes into account the correlation of dependent variables, it is more powerful than ANOVA. The dependent variables for MANOVA must be combined based on **strong theoretical** or **empirical rationales**. One common type I error problem within univariate research is the multiple use of several univariate tests like ANOVA. For example, if one were interested in comparing two groups of participants on five dependent variables of hypnotizability, it would take 5 separate ANOVAs to analyze these data, but the overall alpha level, if it were at the .05 level, would be .05 times the number of separate ANOVAS (5) or about .25; thus, the use of multiple ANOVAs, like the use of multiple t-tests, will increase the chance of type I error.

Hotelling's T squared is the squared multivariate generalization of the t test. The univariate t test is the following:

$$t = \frac{\bar{y}_1 - \bar{y}_2}{\sqrt{\frac{(n_1-1)s_1^2 + (n_2-1)s_2^2}{n_1+n_2-2}\left(\frac{1}{n_1}+\frac{1}{n_2}\right)}}$$

Hoteling's T^2 is the following:

$$T^2 = \frac{n_1 n_2}{n_1 + n_2}(\bar{y}_1 - \bar{y}_2)' S^{-1}(\bar{y}_1 - \bar{y}_2)$$

$(\bar{y}_1 - \bar{y}_2)'$ transpose of vector of means
S- sample covariance matrix
S^{-1} matrix analogue of division is inversion
$(\bar{y}_1 - \bar{y}_2)$ vectors of means

The connection between Hotelling's T^2 and F is the following:

$$F = \frac{n_1 + n_2 - p - 1}{(n_1 + n_2 - 2)p} T^2$$

This formula shows that T^2 provides a F distribution with p and (N-P-1) degrees of freedom. The p is the number of dependent variables and N equals the sample size. Essentially, T^2 is the comparison of between variability divided by within variability.

The univariate d and Mahalanobis distance (D^2) are the following:

univariate $\qquad\qquad$ multivariate

$$d = \frac{\bar{y}_1 - \bar{y}_2}{s} \qquad D^2 = (\bar{y}_1 - \bar{y}_2)' S^{-1}(\bar{y}_1 - \bar{y}_2)$$

D2 is also the following two formulas:

univariate $\qquad\qquad$ multivariate

$$d = \frac{\bar{y}_1 - \bar{y}_2}{s} \qquad D^2 = (\bar{y}_1 - \bar{y}_2)' S^{-1}(\bar{y}_1 - \bar{y}_2)$$

This is formula one.

$$[(n_1 + n_2)/n_1 n_2] T^2$$

This is formula two.

$$\frac{1}{1-r^2}\left[\frac{(x_{i1} - \bar{x}_1)^2}{s_1^2} + \frac{(x_{i2} - \bar{x}_2)^2}{s_2^2} - \frac{2r(x_{i1} - \bar{x}_1)(x_{i2} - \bar{x}_2)}{s_1 s_2}\right]$$

Formula two, clearly show how D^2 takes into account the correlation of these variables.

And T² is the following:

$$[n_1 n_2 / (n_1 + n_2)] D^2$$

Stevens (2002) stated that values of .25 are small effect sizes, values of .5 are medium effect sizes, and values greater than one are large effect sizes. Unlike univariate statistics, Mahalanobis distance takes into account the intercorrelation of variables. Sapp, Obiakor, Gregas, and Scholze (2007) and Pituch and Stevens (2016) described how to calculate Mahalanobis statistic with SPSS.

Let us consider a two-group problem for Hotelling's T². Suppose two forms of treatment – Person-Centered and Rational Emotive Behavior Therapy (REBT) hypnosis – are used to reduce state anxiety and trait anxiety in college students. There are three participants in the Person-Centered group and six in the REBT hypnosis group. State and trait anxiety has a mean of 50 and a standard deviation of 10.

> The following are the SPSS codes for these fictitious data:
> Title 'Two-Group Manova'.
> Data list free/gp dep1 dep2.
> 1 51 53
> 1 53 57
> 1 52 52
> 2 54 56
> 2 56 58
> 2 56 58
> 2 55 60
> 2 55 60
> 2 54 66
> End data.
> Manova dep1 dep2 by gp(1,2)/
>   Print=cellinfo(means)/.

The following selected output from SPSS has the results of Hotelling's T²:

EFFECT .. gp
Multivariate tests of Significance (S = 1, M = 0, N = 2)

Test Name	Value	Exact F. Hypoth.	DF	Error DF	Sig. of F
Pillais	.80855	12.66972	2.00	6.00	.007
Hotellings	4.22324	12.66972	2.00	6.00	.007
Wilks	.19145	12.66972	2.00	6.00	.007
Roys	.80855				

Note. . F statistics are exact.

The following selected output from SPSS has the results of Hotelling's T^2:

EFFECT .. gp
Multivariate tests of Significance (S = 1, M = 0, N = 2)

Test Name	Value	Exact F. Hypoth.	DF	Error DF	Sig. of F
Pillais	.80855	12.66972	2.00	6.00	.007
Hotellings	4.22324	12.66972	2.00	6.00	.007
Wilks	.19145	12.66972	2.00	6.00	.007
Roys	.80855				

Note. . F statistics are exact.

$D^2 = N (T^2) /n_1 n_2 = 9 (4.22)/18 = 2.11$, and this is a large effect size.

Unlike univariate statistics, Mahalanobis distance takes into account the intercorrelation of variables. D^2 is known within a regression context to locate outliers on predictors, and a large value suggests an outlier on a predictor.

Stevens (2007) provided power values for D^2, and he found for values of $D^2 \leq .64$ and $n \leq 25$, power is usually poor (<.45) and seldom adequate >.70. Usually researchers will report the multivariate T^2, and one can calculate D^2 using equation 7. In summary, Mahalanobis distance, or D^2, is the multivariate analogue of the univariate d effect size. Stevens (2002) provided the following guidelines for interpreting D^2:

$$D^2 = .25 \text{ (small effect)}$$
$$D^2 = .5 \text{ (medium effect)}$$
$$D^2 = >1 \text{ (large effect)}$$

DISCUSSION

Mahalanobis distance (D^2) is a multivariate measure of effect, and it is a multivariate measure of distance. For example, large values of D^2 indicate large effect sizes. To summarize:

$$D_i^2 = (\mathbf{X}_1 - \overline{\mathbf{X}})' \mathbf{S}^{-1} (\mathbf{X}_1 - \overline{\mathbf{X}})'$$

D^2 is defined in terms of the covariance matrix of S. X_i equals the vector of the data for case i, and $\overline{\mathbf{X}}$ is the vector of means, or as statisticians call the centroid for predictors within the regression context. D^2 is essential for improving research, and it can be helpful in locating outliers and influential data points in regression analysis (Pituch & Stevens, 2016). Confidence intervals for D^2 is an area for additional research. For example, Hess, Hogarty, Ferron, and Kromney (2007) found that confidence intervals for D^2 were large and uninformative, and they presented SAS/IML code employed in a macro called D2BAND and for these intervals. Mahalanobis distance is a multivariate measure of effect, and it can improve research. Finally, eta squared, the correlation measure of effect, can be used with MANOVA designs.

Chapter 10

MODERATION AND MEDIATION EFFECTS

Moderation and mediation are confusing terms due to their colloquial meanings. From a research methods standpoint, moderating variables are specific types of independent variables that moderate the effects between the primary independent and dependent variables. Moderating variables can be measured, manipulated, and chosen for a study. Levels of motivation and intelligence are moderating variables that can influence the results of test anxiety. In addition, the social learning concept called locus of control can affect test anxiety. Here, locus of control is a generalized expectancy where a student's expectations affect test anxiety. Any factorial ANOVA tests for moderation. Actually, the interaction effect is the test for moderation. Moderation can answer the question of for whom a variable moderates or interacts with a predictor to produce an outcome variable or dependent variable.

Mediation effects are theoretical variables that determine the how and why a relationship exists between an independent variable and dependent variable (Heppner, Wampold, & Kivilighan, 2008). Within the area of test anxiety, the stereotype-threat hypothesis sometimes explains the underperformance of minority students and women in academic settings. The stereotype-threat is the anxiety that one feels when his or her performance will be evaluated based on negative stereotypes. Steeles' (1997) social psychological theory of stereotype threats explains why mediating variables can affect achievement with minorities and women (Sapp, 2014). Heppner, Wampold, Owen, Thompson, and Wang (2016) stated that there are four conditions for mediation. The beta weight or path coefficient between the predictor variable and dependent variable must be statistically significant. Second, the beta weight or path coefficient between the predictor variable and mediator variable must be statistically significant. Third, the beta weight or path coefficient between the mediator variable and dependent variables must be statistically significant. Fourth, the previously statistically significant relationship between the predictor variable and dependent variable is significantly reduced when the mediator variable is added to the analysis or model. Complete mediation occurs when the beta weight or path coefficient between the predictor variable and dependent variable does not differ statistically from zero when the mediator variable is added to the analysis or model. If the path coefficient or path between the predictor variable and dependent variable relationship is reduced when the mediation variable is added to the analysis or model, but still remains statistically significantly different from zero partial mediation is said to have occurred.

Hayes (2013) has a program that can run moderation analyses and mediation analyses using a regression-based approach. Hayes' Process analysis program can be downloaded from the following web address: www.afhayes.com. In addition, Andy Field (2013) has a great video on YouTube called "Moderation and Mediation", and he walks one through both analyses and how to use Hayes' program. When one downloads Hayes' program, it has to be unzipped and has to be run as an administrator on SPSS. Theoretically, through moderation, a moderator interacts with a predictor or X variable to produce changes on the outcome or dependent variable. Readers may be aware that one can put an interaction term X*M into a regression equation in SPSS, but Hayes' program is much easier. Once the program is installed, go to the Analysis Regression menus and the Process program will be in the dialup box. Hayes' program can run 74 different models; he recommends conditional process analysis for moderation-mediation research designs, and he believes in combining both analyses together which is complex and readers can consult his book. With the example that follows, only a simple moderation analysis and a simple mediation analysis will be performed. Colleagues often argue over which analysis should be used for such design, so I recommend that both should be performed. When running the moderation analysis, within the options section, check the mean center products, heteroscedasticity, OSL/ML confidence intervals, and generate data for plotting options. The Johnson-Neyman model allows one to probe an interaction. The Process program uses an interactive or boot strapping process to produce results, so it may take several moments before one receives results.

Finally, Process will abbreviate variable names to eight characters, so make sure that your variable names are not the same when they are shortened.

The following example, taken from Mackinnon (2008), will be used for moderation and mediation using Andrew F. Hayes Process Procedure for SPSS.

X	M	Y
70.00	4.00	3.00
71.00	4.00	3.00
69.00	1.00	3.00
70.00	1.00	3.00
71.00	3.00	3.00
70.00	4.00	2.00
69.00	3.00	3.00
70.00	5.00	5.00
70.00	4.00	4.00
72.00	5.00	4.00
71.00	2.00	2.00
71.00	3.00	4.00
70.00	5.00	5.00
71.00	4.00	5.00
71.00	4.00	5.00
70.00	2.00	2.00
70.00	4.00	4.00
69.00	3.00	5.00
72.00	3.00	4.00
71.00	3.00	3.00
71.00	2.00	4.00
72.00	3.00	5.00
67.00	1.00	2.00
71.00	4.00	4.00
71.00	3.00	2.00
70.00	3.00	4.00
70.00	2.00	3.00
69.00	3.00	4.00
69.00	4.00	3.00
70.00	3.00	3.00
71.00	2.00	1.00
70.00	1.00	3.00
70.00	2.00	5.00

70.00	2.00	1.00
71.00	4.00	3.00
68.00	2.00	1.00
72.00	4.00	3.00
69.00	3.00	2.00
70.00	3.00	3.00
68.00	3.00	2.00
68.00	3.00	3.00
70.00	4.00	3.00
71.00	4.00	4.00
69.00	2.00	2.00
69.00	3.00	3.00
71.00	3.00	4.00
71.00	4.00	4.00
71.00	3.00	2.00
72.00	4.00	5.00
70.00	2.00	2.00

The following are the results from the moderation analysis:

$$Model = 1$$
$$Y = Y$$
$$X = X$$
$$M = M$$

Sample size
50

Outcome: Y

Model Summary

R	R-sq	MSE	F	df1	df2	p
.5274	.2782	.9904	6.2937	3.0000	46.0000	.0011

Model

	coeff	se	t	p	LLCI	ULCI
constant	3.2272	.1582	20.4007	.0000	2.9087	3.5456
M	.4542	.1599	2.8398	.0067	.1323	.7762
X	.2139	.1385	1.5447	.1293	-.0649	.4928
int_1	**.0299**	**.1039**	**.2880**	**.7746**	**-.1791**	**.2390**

The int_1 tests the interaction which was not significant since the p value equals .7746. The readers should remember that p has to be less .05 for statistical significance. In addition, as you will see through your print, the lower limit for interaction effect was -.1791 and the upper limit was .2390. The LLCI denotes the lower limit for the confidence interval and ULCI denotes the upper limit for the confidence interval around the interaction effect. Since zero is contained with the confidence interval, a statistically significant interaction was not found.

The following are the main results from the mediation analysis:

$$Model = 4$$
$$Y = Y$$
$$X = X$$
$$M = M$$

Sample size
50

Outcome: M

Model Summary

R	R-sq	MSE	F	df1	df2	p
.3709	.1376	.9490	7.6564	1.0000 4	8.0000	.0080

Model

	coeff	se	t	p
constant	-20.7024	8.5888	-2.4104	.0198
X	**.3386***	.1224	2.7670	.0080

Outcome: Y

Model Summary

R	R-sq	MSE	F	df1	df2	p
.5265	.2772	.9707	9.0133	2.0000	47.0000	.0005

Model

	coeff	se	t	p
constant	-12.7129	9.1969	-1.3823	.1734
M	**.4510****	.1460	3.0899	.0034
X	.2076	.1333	1.5582	.1259

──────────────────────TOTAL EFFECT MODEL──────────────────────
Outcome: Y

Model Summary

R	R-sq	MSE	F	df1	df2	p
.3611	.1304	1.1435	7.1977	1.0000	48.0000	.0100

Model

	coeff	se	t	p
constant	-22.0505	9.4279	-2.3388	.0236
X	.3604	.1343	2.6829	.0100

──────────────TOTAL, DIRECT, AND INDIRECT EFFECTS──────────────

Total effect of X on Y

Effect	SE	t	p
.3604	.1343	2.6829	.0100

Direct effect of X on Y

Effect	SE	t	p
.2076	.1333	1.5582	.1259

Indirect effect of X on Y

	Effect	Boot SE	BootLLCI	BootULCI
M	.1527	.0648	.0548	.3112

Partially standardized indirect effect of X on Y

	Effect	Boot SE	BootLLCI	BootULCI
M	.1346	.0548	.0506	.2654

Completely standardized indirect effect of X on Y

	Effect	Boot SE	BootLLCI	BootULCI
M	.1530	.0654	.0523	.3120

Ratio of indirect to total effect of X on Y

	Effect	Boot SE	BootLLCI	BootULCI
M	.4238	.8949	.1111	1.8368

Ratio of indirect to direct effect of X on Y

	Effect	Boot SE	BootLLCI	BootULCI
M	.7355	130.9080	-1.3144	24.6675

R-squared mediation effect size (R-sq_med)

	Effect	Boot SE	BootLLCI	BootULCI
M	.0931	.0557	.0068	.2436

Preacher and Kelley (2011) Kappa-squared

	Effect	Boot SE	BootLLCI	BootULCI
M	.1540	.0629	.0532	.3083

——————————ANALYSIS NOTES AND WARNINGS——————————

Number of bootstrap samples for bias corrected bootstrap confidence intervals:
1000

Level of confidence for all confidence intervals in output:
95.00

——————————————————END MATRIX——————————————————

Remember that a mediator variable is a variable that is related to the predictor variable (X variable in this example) and the outcome variable or dependent variable, and the mediator variable explains the relationship between the predictor variable and outcome or dependent variable. The p value for the relationship between the predictor variable and outcome variable Y was .0080 which supports the first condition of mediation. This indicates that there is a statistically significant relationship between the predictor variable and the outcome or dependent variable Y. Another condition of mediation is that the relationship between the predictor variable and outcome variable will reduce or weaken when the mediator variable is entered into the analysis. The p value for the relationship between the predictor variable Y and the outcome variable Y after M the mediator is entered into the analysis was .1259. This indicated the relationship between X and Y went from being statistically significant to none statistically significant or reduced or weakened. The direct effect is the relationship between X and Y, and this effect was reduced to zero when the mediation variable was put into the regression equation. The most important part of this analysis is the indirect effect of X on Y, and these results were .0548 for the lower limit for a 95% confidence interval and .3112 for the upper limit. The lower limited is indicated as "BootLLCI" and the upper limited is noted by "BootULCI." Finally, the coefficient for M or mediation was

.4510 and for X was .2076. The coefficient for M was significant at the .0034 level. Essentially, X coefficient went from .3386 which was statistically significant to .2076 which was not statistically significant; hence, a reduction in this coefficient due to the mediation variable. Mediation analysis can be understood as a path model. The direct effect is X------→Y. This is just the relationship between the predictor and the dependent expressed as a regression coefficient, path coefficient, or beta weight, and this value was .3386. The relationship between the meditator and the dependent variables was .4510. The indirect effect is X----→M----→Y. Here, the path coefficients are multiplied XM. Therefore, .3386(.4510)=.1527086, and the is the same value on the print out rounded to four decimal places(.1527).

Chapter 11
POWER ANALYSIS

There are three concepts related to hypothesis testing; they are Type I error, Type II error, and power. **Type I error** is the level of significance chosen by a clinician or researcher to test the significance of a given statistical test. Type I error, is the probability of wrongly rejecting the null hypothesis (no treatment effect) or the probability of rejecting the null hypothesis when it is true (Stevens, 1999). In effect, with Type I error one is saying that the groups differ, when in fact they do not. **Type II error** is the probability of accepting the null hypothesis when it is false. For example, we are saying the groups do not differ when in fact they do.

The reader should note that Type I and Type II errors are inversely related; that is, as one controls Type I error, Type II error increases, and as one controls Type II error, Type I error increases. Now, power is the probability within statistical or hypothesis testing of rejecting the null hypothesis when it is false; in essence, **power** is the probability of making a correct decision. As Sapp (1997) noted, Type II error and power are related, because power equals one minus Type II errors; therefore, if a clinician or researcher chooses a small alpha level, Type II error increases and power decreases. In fact, it may not be wise to choose an extremely small alpha level such as .01 or .001, since these values tend to reduce statistical power and inflate Type II error. In summary, meta-analysis and its statistics, called effect size measures, allow a clinician or researcher to determine the degree of effect a treatment has within a population, and it determines the degree to which the null hypothesis may be false. There are two estimates of power-a priori and post hoc.

A PRIORI AND POST HOC ESTIMATIONS OF POWER

A priori calculation of power occurs when a researcher estimates power before conducting a study. Here, a researcher can determine the number of participants needed to have power at a certain level. This is especially important before conducting a large study. Post hoc estimation of power is conducting a power analysis after a study has been completed. This writer has found that these two calculations of power can differ greatly. G*Power is a free statistical program that can be found by doing a Google search and downloading the program. G*Power can perform a priori and post hoc estimation of power. G*Power can calculate power for t-tests, Chi-Square tests, F-tests, correlation and regression tests. In addition, it can handle a variety of non-parametric statistics such the Wilcox signed-rank test (match pairs), Wilcox signed-rank test (one sample), and Wilcox-Mann-Whitney test (two groups). G*Power can handle a variety of research designs such as ANOVA, ANCOVA, MANOVA, and repeated measures designs. To use G*Power, a calculated or estimated effect size is needed.

Let me demonstrate how to use G*Power for a post hoc power estimation for a one-way ANOVA design. Suppose we have 10 participants randomly assigned to three groups, and F value equaled 4.38. What would the post hoc power be at an alpha of .05? Within G*Power go "ANOVA: Fixed effects, omnibus one-way" menu and click on "post hoc: Compute achieved power given alpha, sample size, and effect size." Enter the F effect size, alpha level of .05, sample=30, and the number of group=3. Now, click on "calculate." The following are the results of this analysis.

F tests -	ANOVA: Fixed effects, omnibus, one-way		
Analysis:	Post hoc: Compute achieved power		
Input:	Effect size f	=	0.54
	α err prob	=	0.05
	Total sample size	=	30
	Number of groups	=	3
Output:	Noncentrality parameter λ	=	8.7480000
	Critical F	=	3.3541308
	Numerator df	=	2
	Denominator df	=	27
	Power (1-β err prob)	=	0.7068447

Notice that power equals 0.7068447. This result means that there is a 70.68447 chance of finding a difference if one were to exist. Stevens (1990) stated that power is adequate when it is greater than .70. Power is excellent when it is greater than .90. With this example, given an F effect size of .54 (large effect size), alpha level of .05, and a sample size of 30, power is adequate. The noncentrality parameter indicated that this is a noncentral F-distribution. Remember, that noncentral distributions are defined by degrees of freedom and their noncentral parameter.

A priori estimation of power is used to determine the number of participants needed to have power at a desired level. Supposed we have a six-group research design with an f effect size of .25 (medium effect size). How many participants are necessary to have power at alpha .05? It will be necessary to click on the a priori menu in G*Power. The following are the results of this analysis:

F tests	ANOVA: Fixed effects, omnibus, one-way		
Analysis:	A priori: Compute required sample size		
Input:	Effect size f	=	0.25
	α err prob	=	0.05
	Power (1-β err prob)	=	0.70
	Number of groups	=	6
Output:	Noncentrality parameter λ	=	10.8750000
	Critical F	=	2.2679405
	Numerator df	=	5
	Denominator df	=	168
	Total sample size	=	174
	Actual power	=	0.7034693

A total sample size of 174 participants are needed at the alpha .05 level to have power of .70. Therefore, 29 participants are needed per group.

Stevens stated that there are number of ways to improve power. Since my research team and I do counseling psychology research, often, we find there is not a strong link between our treatments and dependent variables. In theory, an independent variable and dependent variable may be related, but during an experiment one may not find a strong link. Sometimes only using one level of an independent variable will improve the link with the dependent variable. For example, sometimes only using females or males in a study may help to improve power by reducing within group variability. Here, homogenous participants tend to vary less on a dependent variable than heterogenous groups. Also, factorial designs can improve statistical power. ANCOVA designs and repeated measures designs can improve power. Multivariate designs are more powerful than univariate research designs.

Chapter 12

PATH ANALYSIS AND EFFECT SIZES

The simplest path analysis or structural equation model is the basic regression equation:

$$Y' = bx + a$$

This equation can be depicted as:

$$X \rightarrow Y \leftarrow e$$

The b or slope is an effect size within a regression context. The straight lines mean that X causes a change on Y, and often these diagrams are called path diagrams. The "e" is the random error caused on Y. The reader should remember that X or the predictor is referred to as the independent variable and Y is the dependent variable. The use of the word "cause" within this context is not a statistical issue, but causality involves logic and research methodology. Bollen (1989) stated that three conditions are necessary, but not enough to imply causality.

First, X must precede Y. Second, X and Y are correlated. Third, no rival hypothesis can account as well for the correlation between X and Y. The reader should remember that conclusions based on structural equation modeling with nonexperimental designs are not as strong as ones obtained from quasi-experimental or preferably true experimental designs. To summarize, structural equation modeling is a theory testing procedure, like planned comparisons, and it must be based on strong theoretical and/or empirical rationales; moreover, they cannot control for threats to internal validity, and structural equations only estimate the causal magnitude of effect if X were truly the cause of Y (McClendon, 1994). With true experimental designs, one is able to state that X caused a change on Y within a certain confidence level or probability range. Finally, causality is not a statistical issue, but a methodological matter.

Path diagrams are used to depict structural models; for example, $X \rightarrow Y$ is called a direct effect, but when a model is mediated by an intervening variable, the model is called an indirect effect. The following depicts an indirect effect: $X_1 \rightarrow X_2 \rightarrow Y$. This model states that X_1 causes a change on X_2 and X_2 causes a change on Y, but X_1 has an indirect effect on Y, since X_2 mediates the relationship between X_1 and Y.

The reader should realize that **path analysis** is a special case of structural equations modeling in which correlations among variables are depicted as graphs (Tabachnick and Fidell, 2001; Sapp, 1999). However, with path analysis, unlike the confirmatory form of factor analysis, the variables are observed and are not latent factors of structures. The reader should remember that with the confirmatory form of structural modeling, latent or unobserved variables are analyzed, but path analysis uses **observed variables**. Suppose we had a theory that a relationship existed among self-esteem, academic self-concept, grades, and reading scores. The following path analysis diagram could depict such a relationship

$$\text{Self-esteem } .62 \rightarrow \text{Academic self-concept} \begin{array}{l} \nearrow .60^* \text{ Grades} \\ \searrow .67^* \text{ Reading Scores} \end{array}$$

*p < .05

The path coefficients are .62, .60, and .67, and these coefficients are **standardized regression coefficients** or beta weights, and are effect sizes. The **direct effect** of self-esteem on academic self-concept is .62, the direct effect of academic self-concept on grades is .60, and the **direct effect** of academic self-concept on reading is .67. **Indirect effects** or **mediation effects** are found by multiplying path coefficients. For example, the indirect effect of self-esteem on grades .62 (.60) = .372, and the indirect effect of self-esteem on reading scores is .62 = .4154. See Chapter 10 for a discussion of mediation effects. Finally, any path coefficient is an effect size.

Finally, the **total effect** is the sum of the direct effects plus the indirect effects. There are certain symbols used with structural equations modeling. For example, an arrow signifies that one variable caused another; rectangular or square boxes signify observed or manifest variables; circles or ellipses signify factors, unobserved variables, or latent variables; and a two-headed arrow signifies the correlation between two variables.

To summarize, structural equation modeling, like simple regression equations, use path diagrams to express relationships among latent variables and measurement errors. Finally, structural equation modeling tests if a sample covariance or correlation matrix differs from a population covariance or correlation matrix, and a non-significant chi-square statistic is used to show support for a structural equation model and a variety of fit indices help determine how well the theoretical model matches actual data.

Chapter 13

FIT INDICES AS EFFECT SIZE MEASURES

Fadlelmula (2011) used a meta-analysis to assess the power of structural equations modeling studies, and he found that power was generally low with these studies. Fadlelmula suggested that the fit indices are effect measures within the structural equations modeling context. Readers may remember that Chi-Squared test is a measure of how well a sample covariance matrix fits a population covariance matrix. A nonsignificant Chi-Squared test indicates a fit between the sample covariance matrix and a population covariance matrix. There are many models of fit within structural equations modeling that are effect size measures.

The Goodness of Fit Index (GFI), the Adjusted Goodness of Fit Index (AGFI), Root Mean Square Error of Approximation (RMSEA), and the Chi-Squared test are the most common effect sizes. The GFI determines how much better a model fits compared to no model at all (Fadlelmula, 2011). Values of the GFI AGFI ranges from 0 to 1, and 0 indicates no fit all and 1 suggests a perfect fit; however, GFI values of .90 or greater indicate a good fit. Similarly, AGFI adjusts the GFI degrees of freedom, and a value of AGFI .90 or greater suggests a good fit. Root Mean Square Residuals (RMR) measure the discrepancies between a theoretical model and observed model, and a value of zero indicates a perfect fit; however, this index is affected by the scale of measurement of the variables, so the Standardized Root Mean Square Residual (S-RMR) is used as an alternative index. S-RMR values of zero is a perfect fit, and 1 indicates a poor fit. In practice, S-RMR values of .05 or less is a good fit, and values of .05 to .10 is an acceptable fit. The Mean Square Error of Approximation (RMSEA) is an analysis of the residuals, and a values of .05 or less is a close fit, and values between .05 to .08 is an adequate fit.

The Normed Fit Index (NFI) has a range from zero to one, and values of .90 or greater is a good fit. Like the NFI, the Incremental Fit Index (IFI) and the Non-Normed Fit Index(NNFI) the Relative Fit Index (RFI), Tucker-Lewis Fit Index (TLI), McDonald's Fit Index (MFI), AGFI, and the Comparative Fit Index (CFI) have a good fit with values .90 or greater. In summary, the NFI, IFI, NNFI, TLI, and CFI are referred to as incremental fit indices and values of .90 are good fits values or recommended cutoff scores. The GFI, AGFI, RMR, S-RMR, and RMSEA are referred to as absolute fit indices. For the GFI, AGFI, and MFI values of .90 or greater indicates a good fit. The S-RMR has a perfect fit with a value of zero, and a value of .05 or less is a good fit. Also, values of S-RMR of .05 to .10 are acceptable fit values. The GFI, AGFI, MFI, S-RMR, and RMSEA are called absolute fit indices (Pitsch & Stevens, 2016). Finally, conceptually, fit indices are effect size measures.

Some researchers confuse reliability and model fit indices, but these concepts are not the same. For example, one can have an acceptable fit model and unacceptable reliability. Even though reliability and model fit are parts of psychometrics, they both have to be tested to determine their acceptability. Also, reliability is the amount of variances account for with a set of items, and it represents a squared correlation, while model fit indices test if a covariance or correlation matrix differ from a population covariance or correlation matrix (Stanley & Edwards, 2016).

BOOK SUMMARY

For years, statisticians have been aware of limits of null hypothesis significance testing (NHST). The Wilkinson Task Force (Wilkinson & Task Force on Statistical Inference, 1999) recommended that researchers report effect sizes and confidence intervals. As indicated in this book, effect sizes started during the 1940s. During this time, correlation effect sizes were proposed. Next, eta, a correlation effect size, was connected to ANOVA, and eta squared was proposed as a variance accounted for effect size. Also, a variant of eta squared, partial eta squared probabilities values were developed in the ANOVA context. The psychologist William L. Hays (1981), in his popular statistics book, proposed omega squared as an alternative to eta squared. Between 1935 to 1963, at least four correlation measures of effect were proposed: eta squared, omega squared, intraclass correlation coefficient, and biserial correlation were proposed by Karl Pearson.

In 1969, Jacob Cohen, proposed an effect size for two group mean differences or comparison. Similar to Cohen, Gene V. Glass proposed a d effect size as the differences between two means divided by the control group standard deviation. Likewise, Larry V. Hedges took exception with Cohen and Glass, and he proposed an adjusted d effect size that he called g Huberty (2002). Moreover, Cohen also proposed a standard mean type differences effect size for multiple group or multiple means within the context of ANOVA. The concept of multiple regression as an effect size was proposed by Pearson and Lee (1897). In this context, the multiple correlation coefficient was a multivariate effect size where participants were measured on two or more predictors and one outcome or dependent variable. Tatsuoka (1970) connected Samuel S. Wilks' (1906–1064) Lambda to the Multivariate Analysis of Variance (MANOVA) as a measure of multivariate strong of association; the smaller the value of Wilks' Lambda, the stronger the multivariate measure of effect (Huberty, 1994). Stevens (1992) proposed a multivariate generalization of Cohen's d effect size. This book covered commonly used univariate and multivariate statistics along with their effect sizes, and connected effect sizes to basic research designs. With the free program G*Power, this book showed how one can conduct a priori calculation of power to determine the number of participants needed to have power at a certain level. G*Power can calculate statistical power for variety of research designs such at t-tests, Chi-Square tests, F-test and correlation and regression tests. Hayes' book and his free program that runs within SPSS and SAS called Process Analysis can run 74 mediation analyses and moderation analyses using a regression-based approach, and he believes in integrating mediation analysis and moderation analysis into one analysis called conditional process analysis.

Whereas multiple regression is the relationship between a set of predictors and a dependent variable, multivariate regression is the relationship between a set of predictors and a set of dependent variables (at least two or more). This book demonstrated how to find an effect size for multiple and multivariate regression. Finally, this book did not emphasize mathematical ability, but statistical software as a means to calculate effect size, confidence intervals, and statistical power for a variety of research designs. This book explained that even the fit indices within structural equations modeling design, are effect sizes.

In terms of resources for calculating effect sizes, the internet has many. For example, one can perform a Google search and find many free resources. For example, Lee Becker at the University of Colorado has a good effect size calculator for the d effect sizes, and he recommends the following correlation effect sizes for ANOVA research designs: eta squared, partial eta squared, omega squared, and the intraclass correlation. His website is located at the following address: http://www.uccs.edu/~lbecker/.

Paul D. Ellis (2010) has good book that covered the essentials of effect sizes and meta-analysis, and Robert J. Grissom and John J. Kim (2005) provided a broad overview of effect sizes. Rex B. Kline (2009) provided an authoritative discussion of the controversy surrounding null hypothesis statistical significance testing. Geoff Cumming (2012) has a good book and a program for calculating effect sizes and confidence intervals. David A. Walker in the *Journal of Modern Applied Statistical Methods* (November, 2015, Vol. 14, No. 2, 282–292), provided algorithms and codes for calculating an array of commonly used effect sizes. Comprehensive Meta-Analysis is one of the simpler programs, and it allows one to use the effect size of one's choice. In addition, completed graphs are provided, fail-safe N statistics. Rosenthal (1979) stated that the fail-safe N is the minimum number of studies needed to overturn the conclusion of a give meta-analysis, and he gave the following equation: fail-safe N=5k+10, k is the number of studies in a meta-analysis. The higher the N, the more confidence one can have in the results of a meta-analysis.

Readers will run into situation where there is missing data when calculating effect sizes. It is important to determine why data is missing. For example, it is important to determine if data is Missing Completely at Random (MCAR), Missing at Random (MAR), or Missing Not At Random (MNAR). Both SPSS and SAS has imputation strategies for missing data. Specifically, imputing means replacing missing data with scores that are reasonable based upon an imputation strategy. It is not a good idea to replace missing data with the mean or some other value not based upon an imputation strategy. If data are Missing At Random (MAR), maximum likelihood estimations can provided unbiased parameter estimates and accurate standard error estimates, and readers can consult Pituch and Stevens (2016) for how to determine the mechanisms and imputation strategies for missing data. This book covered more than 25 effect sizes that were connected to simple research designs; however, a researcher or clinician has to apply a reasonable thought process to determine which effect may be useful for his or her research.

REFERENCES

Bird, K. D. (2002). Confidence intervals for effect sizes in analysis of variance. *Educational and Psychological Measurement, 62,* 197–226.

Bollen, K. A. (1989). *Structural equations with latent variables.* New York: Wiley.

Bryant, F. B. (2000). Assessing the validity of measurement. In L. G. Grimm & P. R. Yarnold (Eds.), *Reading and understanding more multivariate statistics* (pp. 99–146). Washington, DC: American Psychological Association.

Cohen, J. (1977). *Statistical power analysis for the behavioral sciences.* New York: Academic Press.

Cohen, J., Cohen, P., West, S. G., & Aiken, L. S. (2003). *Applied multiple regression/correlation analysis for the behavioral sciences* (3rd ed.). Mahwah, NJ: Lawrence Erlbaum.

Cook, T. D. (2008). "Waiting for life to arrive": A history of the regression-discontinuity design in psychology, statistics and economics. *Journal of Econometrics, 142*(2), 636–654.

Cumming, G. (2012). Understanding the new statistics: Effect size, confidence intervals, and meta-analysis. New York: Routledge.

Ellis, P. D. (2010). *The essential guide to effect sizes: Statistical power, meta-analysis, and the interpretation of research results.* Cambridge: Cambridge University Press.

Fadlelmula, F. K. (2011). Assessing power of structural equation modeling studies: a meta-analysis. *Education Research Journal, 1*(3), 37–42.

Ferguson, C. J. (2009). An effect size primer: A guide for clinicians and researchers. *Professional Psychology: Research and Practice, 40*(5), 532-538.

Fidler, F., Cumming, G. Thomason, N., Pannuzzo, D., Fyffe, P., Edmonds, H., Harrington, C. & Schmitt, R. (2005). Toward improved statistical reporting in the Journal of Consulting and Clinical Psychology. *Journal of Consulting and Clinical Psychology, 73*(1), 136–143.

Field, A. (2013). *Discovering statistics using IBM SPSS statistics.* Newbury Park, CA: Sage.

Fisher, R. A. (1928). *Statistical methods for research workers* (2nd ed.). London: Oliver and Boyd.

Green, B. F., & Hall, J. A. (1984). Quantitative methods for literature reviews.

Annual review of psychology, 35(1), 37–54. *Understanding more multivariate statistics.* Washington, DC: American Psychological Association.

Grimm, L. G., & Yarhold, P. R. (Eds.). (2002) *Reading and understanding more multivariate statistics.* Washington, DC: American Psychological Association.

Grissom, R. J., & Kim, J. J. (2005). *Effect sizes for research: A broad practical approach.* Mahwah, NJ: Lawrence Erlbaum.

Harwell, M. (1998). Misinterpreting interaction effects in analysis of variance. *Measurement and Evaluation in Counseling and Development, 37*(2) 125-136.

Hayes, A. F. (2013). *Introduction to mediation, moderation, and conditional process analysis: A regression-based approach.* New York, NY: Guilford Press.

Hays, W. (1981). *Statistics* (3rd ed.). New York: Holt, Rinehart, & Winston.

Helms, J. E., Henze, K. T., & Sass, T. L. (2006). Treating Cronbach's alpha reliability coefficients as data in counseling research. *The Counseling Psychologist, 34*(5), 630–660.

Heppner, P. P., Wampold, B. E., Owen, J., Thompson, M.N, & Wang, K.T. (2016). Research design in counseling. Boston, MA: *Cengage Learning.*

Huberty, C. J. (2002). A history of effect sizes. *Educational and Psychological Measurement, 62*(2), 227–240.

Huitema, B. (1980). *The analysis of covariance and alternatives.* New York: Wiley.

Hunter, J. E., & Schmidt, F. L. (1990). *Methods of meta-analysis: Correcting error and bias in research findings.* Newbury Park: CA: Sage.

Kahn, J. H. (2006). Factor analysis in counseling psychology research, training, and practice: Principles, advances, and applications. *The Counseling Psychologist,* 34(5), 684-718.

Keppel, G. (1983). *Design and analysis: A researcher's handbook.* Englewood Cliffs, NJ: Prentice-Hall.

Kirk, R. (1995). *Experimental design: Procedures for the behavioral sciences* (3rd ed.). Pacific Grove, CA: Brooks/Cole.

Kirk, R. (1982). *Experimental design: Procedures for the behavioral sciences.* Belmont, CA: Brooks-Cole.

Kline, R. B. (2005). *Principles and practices of structural equation modeling* (2nd ed.). New York: Guildford Press.

Kline, R. B. (2009). Becoming a behavioral science researcher: A guide to producing research that matters. NY; The Guildford Press.

Kline, R. B. (2004). *Beyond significance testing: Reforming data analysis methods in behavioral research.* Washington, DC: American Psychological Association.

Lancaster, B. P. (1999). Defining and interpreting suppressor effects: Advantages and limitations. In B. Thompson (Ed.), *Advances in social science methodology* (Vol. 5, pp. 139–148). Stamford, CT: JAI Press.

Lindman, H. R. (1991). *Analysis of variance in experimental design.* New York: Springer-Verlag.

MacKinnon, D. P. (2008). *Introduction to statistical mediation analysis.* New York: Routledge.

Menard, S. (2002). *Applied logistic regression analysis* (No. 106). Newbury Park, CA: Sage.

Pampel, F. C. (2000). *Logistic regression: A primer* (Vol. 132). Newbury Park, CA: Sage.

Pedhazur, E. J. (1997). *Multiple regression in behavioral research: Explanation and prediction* (3rd ed.). Fort Worth, TX: Harcourt Brace.

Pituch, K. A., & Stevens, J. P. (2016). *Applied multivariate statistics for the social sciences: Analyses with SAS and IBM's SPSS.* New York: Routledge.

Rhoads, C. H., & Dye, C. (2016). Optimal design for two-level random assignment and regression discontinuity studies. The Journal of Experimental Education, 84(3), 421-448.

Rosenthal, R. (1984). *Meta-analytic procedures for social research.* Beverly Hills, CA: Sage.

Rosenthal, R. (1979). The "file drawer problem" and tolerance for null results. *Psychological Bulletin, 86,* 638–641.

Rosenthal, R., & Rosnow, R. L. (1984). *Understanding behavioral science.* New York: McGraw-Hill.

Rosenthal, R., Rosnow, R. L., & Rubin, D. B. (2000). *Contrasts and effect sizes in behavioral research: A correlational approach.* Cambridge: Cambridge University Press.

Sapp, M. (2015). *Hypnosis, dissociation, and absorption: Theories, assessment, and treatment.* Springfield, IL: Charles C Thomas.

Sapp, M. (2014). *Test anxiety: Applied research, assessment, and treatment interventions* (3rd ed.). Lanham, MD: University Press of America.

Sapp, M. (2006). *Basic psychological measurement, research design, and statistics without out math.* Spirngfield, IL: Charles C Thomas.

Sapp, M. (2004a). *Cognitive-behavioral theories of counseling: Traditional and nontraditional approaches.* Springfield, IL: Charles C Thomas.

Sapp, M. (2004b). Confidence intervals within hypnosis research. *Sleep and Hypnosis, 6*(4), 169-176

Sapp, M. (2002). *Psychological and educational test scores: What are they?* Springfield, IL: Charles C Thomas.

Sapp, M. (1999). *Test anxiety: Applied research, assessment, and treatment intervention* (2nd ed.). Lanham, MD: University Press of America.

Sapp, M. (1997). *Counseling and psychotherapy: Theories, associated research, and issues.* Lanham, MD: University Press of America.

Sapp, M., Obiakor, F. E., Gregas, A., & Scholze, S. (2007). Mahalanobis Distance: A multivariate measure of effect in hypnosis research. *Sleep and Hypnosis, 9*(2), 67–70.

Shadish, W. R., Cook, T. D., & Campbell, D. T. (2002). *Experimental and quasi-experimental designs for generalized causal inference.* Wadsworth Cengage learning.

Siegel, S. (1956). *Nonparametric statistics for the behavioral sciences.* New York: McGraw-Hill.

Siegel, S., & Castellan, N. J. (1988). *Nonparametric statistics for the behavioral sciences* (2nd ed.). New York: McGraw-Hill.

Smithson, M. (2003). *Confidence intervals.* Thousand Oaks, CA: Sage.

Smithson, M. (2001). Correct confidence intervals for various regression effect sizes and parameters: The importance of noncentralized distributions in computing intervals. *Educational and Psychological Measurement, 61,* 605–632.

SPSSX user's guide (3rd ed.). (1988). Chicago: SPSS, Inc.

Stanley, L. M., & Edwards, M. C. (2016). Reliability and model fit. *Educational and Psychological Measurement, 76*(6), 976–985.

Steiger, J. H., & Fouladi, R. T. (1997). Noncentrality interval estimation and the evaluation of statistical models. In L. Harlow, S. Malaik, & J. H. Steiger (Eds.), *What if there were no significance tests?* (pp. 222–257). Hillsdale, NJ: Lawrence Erlbaum Associates.

Steele, C. M. (1997). A threat in the air: How stereotypes shape intellectual identity and performance. *American psychologist, 52*(6), 613.

Steiger, J. H., & Fouladi, R. T. (1992). R2: A computer program for interval estimation, power calculation, and hypothesis testing for the squared multiple correlation. *Behavior Research Methods, Instruments, and Computer, 4,* 581–582.

Stevens, J. P. (2002). *Applied multivariate statistics for the social sciences* (4th ed.). Mahwah, NJ: Lawrence Erlbaum.

Stevens, J. P. (1999). *Intermediate statistics: A modern approach* (2nd ed.). Mahwah, NJ: Lawrence Erlbaum

Stevens, J. P. (1980). Power of the multivariate analysis of variance tests. *Psychological Bulletin, 88*(3), Nov 1980, 728–737.

Stevens, J. (1990). *Intermediate statistics: A modern approach.* Hillsdale, NJ: Lawrence Erlbaum.

Tabachnick, B. G., Fidell, L. S., & Osterlind, S. J. (2001). *Using multivariate statistics.* New York: Person.

Thompson, B. (2004). *Exploratory and confirmatory factor analysis: Understanding concepts and applications.* Washington, D.C.: American Psychological Association.

Thompson, B. (2003). *Score reliability: Contemporary thinking on reliability issues.* Thousand Oaks, CA: Sage.

Thompson, B. (2002). "Statistical," "practical," and "clinical": How many kinds of significance do counselors need to consider? *Journal of Counseling and Development, 80,* 64–71.

Thompson, B. (1995). Exploring the replicability of a study's results: Bootstrap statistics for the multivariate case. *Educational and Psychological Measurement, 55*, 84–94.

Thompson, B. (1994). Guidelines for authors. *Educational and Psychological Measurement, 54*, 837–847.

Thompson, B. (1992). Two and one-half decades of leadership in measurement and evaluation. *Journal of Counseling and Development, 70*, 434-438.

Thompson, B., & Borrello, G. M. (1985). The importance of structure coefficients in regression research. *Educational and Psychological Measurement, 45*, 203–209.

Vogt, W. P., & Johnson, B. R. (2011). *Dictionary of statistics and methodology: A nontechnical guide for the social sciences* (4th ed.). Thousand Oaks, CA: Sage.

Vogt, W. P. (1999). *Dictionary of statistics and methodology: A nontechnical guide for the social sciences.* Thousand Oaks, CA: Sage.

Wang, Z., & Thompson, B. (2007). Is the Pearson r 2 biased, and if so, what is the best correction formula?. *The Journal of Experimental Education, 75*(2), 109-125.

Wilkinson Task Force on Statistical Inference. (1999). Statistical methods in psychology journals: Guidelines and explanations. *American Psychologist, 54*, 594-604.

Wolf, F. M. (1986). *Meta-analysis: Quantitative methods for research synthesis* (Vol. 59). Thousand Oaks, CA: Sage.

NAME INDEX

A

Aiken, L. S., 122, 130

B

Beck, A., 49
Becker, L., 166
Bird, K. D., 35, 36, 49
Bollen, K. A., 160
Borrello, G. M., 17
Bounds, W. G., 104, 125
Bryant, F. B., 15, 16, 17, 22

C

Campbell, D. T., 67, 104
Cohen, J., 4, 5, 6, 7, 8, 23, 24, 25, 35, 40, 42, 48, 76, 101, 107, 122, 130, 165
Cohen, P., 122, 130
Cook, T. D., 66, 67, 104
Cormier, W. H., 104, 125
Cramer, 46, 109–110, 111–112, 113, 114
Cumming, G., 36, 47, 48, 49, 166

D

Dye, C., 66

E

Edmunds, H., 36
Edwards, M. C., 164
Ellis, A., 49
Ellis, P., 166

F

Fadlelmula, F. K., 163
Ferguson, C. J., 23, 24, 27, 46, 47, 59, 121
Ferron, J. M., 147
Fidell, L. S., 161
Fidler, F., 36
Field, A., 122, 135–136, 149
Finch, J., 48, 54
Fisher, R. A., 4, 28, 29, 39, 42–44, 43t–44t, 48, 72
Fouladi, R. T., 31, 53
Freud, S., 50
Fyffe, P., 36

G

Glass, J. V., 5, 24, 46, 165
Green, B. F., 42
Gregas, A., 28, 59, 145
Grissom, R. J., 166

H

Hall, J. A., 42
Harrington, C., 36
Harwell, M., 84
Hayes, A. F., 4, 149, 150, 165
Hays, W. L., 4, 84, 164
Hedges, L. V., 5, 23, 24, 41, 165
Heins, K. T., 13
Helms, J. E., 13
Heppner, P. P., 148
Herzberg, P. A., 131
Hess, M. R., 147
Hogarty, K. Y., 147
Hopkins, K. D., 46
Howitt, D. L., 113

Huberty, C. J., 3, 5, 8, 165
Huck, S. W., 104, 125
Huitema, B., 101, 102
Hunter, J. E., 46

J

Johnson, B. R., 17

K

Kahn, J. H., 19
Kelley, T., 4
Keppel, G., 90, 98
Kim, J. J., 166
Kirk, R., 90
Kivligham, D. M., 148
Kline, R. B., 53, 54, 125, 166
Kromney, J. D., 147

L

Lancaster, B. P., 128–129
Lee, A., 8, 165
Lindman, H. R., 72
Lyman, H. B., 15, 18

M

McClendon, M. J., 160
Menard, S., 135–136

O

Obiakor, F. E., 28, 59, 145
Owen, J., 148

P

Pampel, F. C., 135–136
Pannuzzo, D., 36
Pearson, K., 4, 8, 165
Pedhazur, E. J., 17, 122, 127, 130
Pituch, K. A., 16, 20, 21, 27, 40, 107, 122, 136, 145, 166

R

Rhoads, C. H., 66
Rosenthal, R., 13, 24, 39, 42, 44–45, 46, 48, 166

Rosnow, R. L., 13, 39, 44–45, 46
Rubin, D. B., 39

S

Sapp, M., 9, 13, 14, 15, 16, 27, 28, 30, 31, 35, 36, 40, 42, 48, 59, 61, 66, 67, 81, 90, 96–97, 101, 103, 122, 124, 129, 145, 148, 156, 161
Sass, T. L., 13
Schmidt, F. L., 46
Schmitt, R., 36
Scholze, S., 28, 59, 145
Shadish, T. R., 67, 104
Siegel, S., 113
Smithson, M., 31, 36, 49
Stanley, L. M., 164
Steele, C. M., 148
Steiger, J. H., 31, 53
Stein, C., 131
Stevens, J. P., 16, 20, 21, 27, 40, 72, 84, 86, 103, 107, 122, 125, 127, 131, 136, 137, 145, 146, 156, 158, 165, 166

T

Tabachnick, B. G., 161
Tatsuoka, M. M., 8
Thomason, N., 36
Thompson, B., 16–17, 20, 28, 35, 36, 59, 121, 124, 128, 129
Thompson, M. N., 148

V

Vogt, W. P., 17, 19, 129, 130

W

Walker, D. A., 166
Wampold, B. E., 148
Wang, K. T., 148
Wang, Z., 36
West, S. G., 122, 130
Wherry, R. J, 131
Wilkinson Task Force on Statistical Inference, v, 164
Wilks, S. S., 8, 140, 165
Wolf, F. M., 41, 46

SUBJECT INDEX

A

ability tests, 15
absolute fit indices, 164
academic self-concept, 161
achievement tests, 15
adjusted cell mean, 83, 84
Adjusted Goodness of Fit Index (AGFI), 163, 164
adjusted R-squared, 131–132, 132t
Adlerian therapy, 50
alpha level, 72, 89, 156
alternative forms reliability, 10, 11
ANCOVA (Analysis of Covariance)
    effect size for, 107
    multivariate generalization of, 25
    one-way, 101–107
    overview of, 101–103
    power, improving through, 159
    SPSS control lines for, 104–107
ANOVA (analysis of variance). *See also* one way ANOVA (analysis of variance).
    advantages of, 72
    ANCOVA compared to, 103
    as case of regression, 120, 120t
    correlation effect sizes for, 166
    eta probability in context of, 4
    eta squared connected to, 3, 76, 164
    formula for, 118
    MANOVA, relationship to, 25, 143
    mixed model, 84
    multivariate extension of, 25
    multivariate tests of significance, 141t
    output, 93t
    power estimate and, 158
    as pre-test and post-test comparison alternative, 103–104
    regression relationship to, 125, 125t
    summary table, examples of, 85t
    sum of squares and, 133t, 134t
    techniques from, 102
anxiety, reducing, 145
a priori power estimate, 156, 157, 158
asymmetrical correlations, 116

B

backward elimination, 124, 132, 132t, 135
balanced (defined), 84
behavioral therapy, 49
behavior modification, 49
beta weight, 121, 129, 130, 135, 161
between group design, 63, 67
between-subjects effects, 76, 85t–86t, 88t
biofeedback, 49
biserial correlation coefficient, 4–5, 109, 165
Bonferroni inequality (test), 72

C

canonical correlation, 17, 130
causality, 160, 161
cause (term), 160
cell interaction effect, 83
central distributions, 53–54
chi squared, 110–111, 114
chi-square statistic, 162
chi square test, 157, 163, 165
classical test theory, 8
coefficient alpha
    confidence intervals for, 33–34, 35
    defined, 9
    as internal consistency measure, 11–12
    multidimensional reliability coefficient of, 13
    as pretest score reliability estimate, 102

coefficient of determination, 15, 131
coefficients
    SPSS control lines for, 120t
    standardized and unstandardized, 134, 134t, 135t
cognitive-behavioral orientations effect sizes for, 49, 50, 52t
cognitive-behavioral therapy
    d effect size for, 50
    defined, 49
    effect size for, 51
    learning as factor in, 130
    upper confidence intervals for, 51
cognitive therapy, 49, 50
column main effect, 80
commonality, 19, 20t
communality (h^2), 19
Comparative Fit Index (CFI), 164
comparisons, 90–95
Comprehensive Meta-Analysis program, 166
concurrent validity, 18
confidence interval. *See also* 95% confidence interval.
    around correlations, 48–49
    around d effect size, 48–49, 53–56, 64–66
    around effect size, v
    around r effect size, 47–53, 52t–53t, 56
    around reliability indices, 35
    around t-test statistic, 68
    around validity, 29–31
    biserial correlation coefficient, relationship to, 5
    calculating, 56, 65, 65t, 165
    counternull hypothesis relationship to, 39
    for d effect size measures, 36
    definition and overview of, 27–28
    limits for, 152
    for Mahalanobis distance (D^2), 147
    one sample case of, 32–34
    as research area, 34–35
    SAT scores, 59–61
confidence level, 161
confirmatory factor analysis, 19, 20
conservative post hoc procedures, 95
constant variance (defined), 119, 126
constructive validity, 18–22
content validity, 15
contrast, 90–91, 92–95, 94t
convergent validity, 22
correlation effect size, 68–69, 164, 166

correlation ratio (correlation eta), 3, 112, 164
correlations
    confidence intervals around, 48–49
    as effect sizes, 108–114, 116–121
    linearity assumption, testing, 116–117
    meta-analysis, use within, 48
    overview and coefficient types, 108–116, 115t
    special cases of, 72–73
    SPSS control lines for, 117t
    test-retest reliability and, 11t
    tests, 157, 165
counseling psychology research, 35, 158
counternull hypothesis, 39
counternull value, 39
course validity (term), 15
covariant matrix, sample, 21
covariate, 16, 108. *See also* independent variable
covert behavioral therapy, 49–50, 51
Cramer's phi, 46, 114
Cramer's phi correlation coefficient, 109–112
creative imagination, 5, 109
criterion validity, 13, 15–16, 18
Crohnbach's alpha. *See* coefficient alpha
cross-validation formulas, 131–135
cross-validation regression equations, 125
curricular validity (term), 15
cutoff-based scores designs, 66

D

D2BAND macro, 147
data, missing, imputation strategies for, 166
data exploration, 91
d effect size
    application of, 41–42
    calculating, 166
    confidence intervals around, 48–49, 53–56, 64–66
    definition and overview of, 5, 23–24, 48, 64
    interpreting, 6
    measures, 36
    meta-analysis, use within, 48
    for pretest posttest design, 68
    proposal of, 165
    psychological research, improving with, 56
    r effect size relationship to, 7

sample data, 24
   of therapies, 50, 52t–53t
   upper limits of, 51
degrees of freedom, 85, 111
DEP, tests of significance for, 98t, 99t
dependent variable
   denoting, 108, 160
   dichotomous, 137
   examples of, 123
   independent variable, relationship to, 158
   predicting, 122
descriptive discriminant analysis, 16–17, 25
desensitization (defined), 49
dichotomous dependent variables, 46
differential validity, 17–18
direct effect (defined), 161
discriminant analysis, 130
discriminant validity, 22
disordinal interaction, 80
disproportional cell size, 86–88
dummy variable (defined), 140
Duncan's new multiple range test, 95
Dunnett's test, 95
dynamic/humanistic therapy, 51

E

effect, 39, 86, 164–165
   effect sizes
      calculating, 76, 107, 165, 166
      classification of, 40–41, 145
      confidence intervals for highest, 53t
      correlations as, 108–114, 116–121
      definition and overview of, 23–25
      fit indices as, v, 163–164, 165–166
      history of, 3–8
      mathematical treatment of, vi
      measures, v, 36, 156, 163–164, 165–166
      meta-analysis, use within, 48
      nested designs, not applicable to, 99
      path analysis and, 160–162
      for predictors and coefficients, 134
      proposal of, 164
      purpose of, v, 36
      as research area, 34–35
      research designs, selecting for, 166–167
      of therapies, 52t–53t
      for two group mean comparisons, 5, 165
      for two-group multivariate analysis of variance, 143–147

ego states, 50
eigenvalue, 13, 21
empirical validity, 15, 18
equality of means, 79
error
   of estimate, 29
   independence of, 118, 119, 126, 127
   of measurement, 28
   in prediction, 117
   standard, 30
   Type I, 40, 72, 95, 156
   Type II, 40, 156
error term, 82, 137
ESCI (Exploratory Software for Confidence Intervals) confidence intervals, calculating with, 65, 65t
eta, 3, 112, 164
eta probability, 4
eta squared
   as ANCOVA effect size, 107
   ANOVA, connection to, 3, 76, 164
   confidence intervals for, 77
   MANOVA designs, use with, 142, 147
   omega squared as alternative to, 4
   proposal of, 164–165
experimental approach to unbalanced factorial design, 86
explained variation, formula for, 117–118
external validity, 14
Ezekiel and Smith r squared corrections, 38

F

face validity, 14
factor analysis, 13, 16, 19, 20, 161
factorial ANOVA (analysis of variance), 86, 148
factorial designs, 80–84, 86–88, 159
factorial validity, 18–19
factor loadings, 17, 19, 20t, 130
fail-safe N statistics, 166
f effect size, 5, 101
first order interaction, 87
Fisher's LSD (Least Significant Difference), 95
Fisher's Z, 28, 29, 39, 48
   transformations of r to z, 42–44, 43t–44t
fit indices, v, 163–164, 165–166
five-way interaction, 89
fixed effects ANOVA (analysis of variance),

84
flooding, 49, 50
forced entry, 123, 124, 136
forward entry, 123–125
forward entry method, 134
four-way interaction, 89
frequency table, 110t
F-statistic, 72–73, 75, 76, 112
F-test
   ANOVA, 158
   calculating, 73
   comparisons performed after, 90
   for contrast, 92–94
   Hotelling's T squared connection to, 144
   interaction, 104
   main effect testing with, 82–83
   normality assumption, robustness to, 126–127
   power for, 157, 165
   significant, follow-up tests to, 95
   univariate, 140, 141t

G

Games-Howell post hoc test for unequal variances, 79–80
Gamma Statistic, 114
Gestalt therapy, 51
GLM (general linear model), 99–101, 125, 141t
Goodness of Fit Index (GFI), 163
G*Power program, 40, 157, 165
grades, 161
group differences indices, 5
grouping variable, 3–4
group mean as unit of analysis, 73
group membership, classifying or discriminating, 16
guided imagery, 49, 50

H

harmonic mean, 96
Hayes' Process analysis program, 149–151, 165
heterogenous participants in group, 159
hierarchical approach to unbalanced factorial design, 86
hierarchical regression (term), 136
homogeneity of variance, test of, 76t, 119
homogenous participants in group, 159
homoscedasticity of variance, 118, 119, 126, 137
Hotelling's T squared, 26, 143–144, 145–146
hypnosis, 49
hypnotherapy, 49, 50, 51
hypnotic susceptibility, 81
hypnotizability, 109, 110t
hypotheses, 91
hypothesis testing, 40, 60, 89, 156
hypothesized values, 28–29
hypotizabiity, 5

I

implosive therapy, 49, 50
incremental fit indices, 164
independent variable, 108, 122, 158, 160
indirect effect (defined), 161
interaction, 80–81, 84, 104, 149
interaction effect
   defined, 80
   limits for, 152
   as moderation effect, 145
   within multiple regression, 130–131
   significance, testing for, 84
   sum of squares and mean square, calculating for, 84
   in unbalanced factorial designs, 86–87
interaction term, calculating, 83
internal consistency, 10, 11–12
internal validity
   defined, 14, 35
   selection threats to, 102–103
   threats to, 68, 101
   threats to, controlling, 35–36, 66
inter-rater (inter-scorer) reliability, 10, 11
intervening variables, 129–130
intraclass correlation coefficient, 4, 165
IQ scores, 28
irrational beliefs, changing, 91–95
item response theory, 136–137

J

Johnson-Neyman model, 149
Johnson-Neyman technique, 103

K

Kappa Coefficient of Agreement, 114
Kendall Coefficient of Concordance, 112–113
Kendall Rank Correlation (Kendall's tau), 112, 116–117, 117t
K group (defined), 140

L

Lambda, 8, 140, 165
Lambda Statistic, 114, 116
largest semipartial, predictor with, 123
learning as moderating variable, 130
least squares multiple regression, 136
Levene's test of homogeneity of variances, 76t, 79t
liberal post hoc procedures, 95
linearity, 118–119, 126
loading, 13, 17, 130
locus of control, 148
logical validity (term), 15
logistic regression, 135–138
log linear analysis, 25
lower-bounds, communalities as, 19

M

Mahalanobis distance (D2), 26–27, 144, 145, 146, 147
main effect, 82–83, 84
MANCOVA (Multivariate Analysis of Covariance), 25
MANOVA (Multivariate Analysis of Variance)
    ANOVA, relationship to, 25, 143
    applications of, 8, 98, 100–101
    eta squared use with, 142, 147
    Lambda, relationship to, 8, 165
    in multivariate regression, 140, 142
    two-group, 143–147
mathematical maximization procedure, 22
maximum likelihood estimation, 136–137
McDonald's Fit Index (TLI), 164
means, 79, 90, 106t
Mean Square Error of Approximation (RMSEA), 163
measurement as research area, 34–35
mediation
    analysis, 152–155
    coefficient for, 154–155
    conditions for, 148–149, 154
    designs, presentation of, v
    effects, 148, 161
mediator variable (defined), 154
medical research, 46–47
meta-analysis, 24, 39–47, 156, 166
minorities, 35, 148
mixed model ANOVA (analysis of variance), 84
model fit indices, 164
modeling, 50, 51
moderating variables, 148
moderation, v, 148, 151–152
MSB (mean square between groups), 73, 74–75, 82–83
MSW (mean squares within), 4, 73–74, 75, 82–83, 84, 85, 107
multidimensional reliabilities, 13
multidimensional scales, reliability for, 13
multiple correlation coefficient, 8
multiple groups, effect size type for, 5
multiple regression
    analysis of, 140
    assumptions of, 126–127
    cross-validation formulas within, 131–135
    definition and overview of, 8, 16, 122, 136, 165
    interaction effects within, 130–131
    predictors significant at level of, 141–142
    structure coefficients within, 130
    sums of squares, breakdown into, 126t
    suppressor variables in, 127–130
multitrait-multimethod, 22
multivariate (defined), 140
multivariate indices, 8
multivariate regression, 139–142, 165
multivariate research design, 159
multivariate statistics, v, 25–27
multivariate tests of significance, 141t, 146t

N

nested ANOVA (analysis of variance), 96–101
Newman-Kuels post hoc procedure, 95
95% confidence interval
    99% confidence interval compared to, 28
    around coefficient alpha, 11–12
    around effect size, 48, 54–56, 66
    around t-test statistic, 69

for eta squared, 77
examples of, 59–61
one sample case of, 32–34
wide use of, 27
99% confidence interval, 27–28, 59
noncentralized distributions, 53, 64–65
nonequivalent control group design, 101–102
Non-Normed Fit Index (NNFI), 164
nonparametric correlations, 117t
normality, assumption of, 118, 119, 126
Normed Fit Index (NFI), 164
null hypothesis
  accepting or rejecting, 36, 51
  for contrast, 92
  examples of, 81–82
  rejecting wrongly, probability of, 40, 56
  truth, assumption of, 53
null hypothesis, false
  accepting wrongly, probability of, 40, 156
  allowing or rejecting, 35
  non-centralized distribution use and, 64
  rejecting, probability of, 48
null hypothesis significance testing (NHST)
  central distribution use in, 53–54
  controversy surrounding, 166
  limits of, v, 35, 164
null hypothesis testing, alternatives to, 90

O

observed variables, path analysis use of, 161
occupational tests, content validity use in, 15
omega squared, 4, 164, 165
one-between ANOVA (analysis of variance), 103–104
one group, confidence interval for effect size d for, 55–56
one-group before-after design (term), 68
one group pretest-posttest design, 68–69, 107
one-sample test, 32–33, 32t, 60–61, 60t
one-way ANCOVA (analysis of covariance), 101–107
one-way ANOVA (analysis of variance)
  calculating, 96
  eta squared and partial eta equared for, 76
  factorial ANOVA compared to, 86
  null hypothesis for, 92
  overview of, 72–75
  results of, 107
  statistical assumptions of, 91

one-way qui square, degrees of freedom for, 111
one within ANOVA (analysis of variance), 103–104
ordinal interaction, 80
overlap indices, 5–6

P

pairwise comparison, 91
part correlation (term), 124
partial correlation, formula for, 123–124
partial eta squared, 76
PASS program, 40
path analysis, 160–162
path diagrams, 160, 161, 162
Pearson correlation coefficient, 5, 11, 11t, 37
Pearson product-moment correlation
  Cramer's phi interpreted as, 112
  definition and overview of, 108
  for dichotomous dependent variables, 46
  distribution of, 30
  familiarity with, 48
  formula for, 24–25
  sampling distribution of, 47
  Spearman Rank Order correlation compared to, 109
  SPSS control lines for, 117t
  as symmetrical correlation, 116
  term usage, 36
Pearson product-moment correlation coefficient, 24
Pearson r (term), 37, 108
personality, constructs of, 50
personality tests, 15
person-centered therapy, 51, 145
pilot success, predicting, 128
planned comparison, 90, 91–95
point biserial correlation coefficient, 109
population characteristics, 27
population correlation coefficient, 47–48
population data, 24
population reliability, 19
postdictive validity, 18
post hoc comparison, 90, 91
post hoc power estimate, 156, 157–158
post hoc procedures, 95–96
post-test, 105t–106t
power
  calculating, 165

defined, 40, 48, 156, 158
estimates of, 156–159
improving, 158, 159
power analysis
  effect size relationship to, 48
  non-centralized distribution importance for, 64
  overview of, 156–159
  performing, 35, 40, 107
  presentation of, v
power values, 51, 53t, 76
predictive validity, 16–18
predictor. *See also* independent variable
  dummy coding of, 140
  effect sizes for, 134
  error in, 29
  examples of, 123, 127–128
  extremes, identifying on, 130–131
  interaction of, 130
  mediator variable relationship to, 154
  selecting, 123–125
  term, 108, 160
  use of, 29
predictor-independent variables (term), 16
pre-test, 106t
pretest-posttest data, 103
pretest-posttest design, 66–67, 68–69, 107
pretests (term), 16
pretest scores, 102
principal-axis factoring, 19
principal components, 20–21
principal components analysis, 13, 19, 20, 21, 22
probability range, 161
propensity score matching, 104
prospective validity (term), 16
psychoanalysis, 50
psychological research, 35, 56
psychotherapy, 50, 53t

Q

quasi-experimental research design, 67
quasi-intervals, 36–37

R

random effects ANOVA (analysis of variance), 84
rational emotive behavior therapy, 91–95

rational emotive behavior therapy hypnosis, 91–95, 145
reading scores, 161
reality therapy, 50, 51
r effect size
  calculating, 38–39, 56
  confidence intervals around, 47–53, 52t–53t
  d effect size relationship to, 7
  definition and overview of, 23, 24, 36–39
  practical significance of, 44–47
  psychological research, improving with, 56
  of therapies, 52t
  types of, 24–25
regression
  ANOVA (analysis of variance) relationship to, 101, 125, 125t
  defined, 122
  as effect size, 108, 121
  special cases of, 72–73, 120, 120t
  techniques from, 102
  tests, 165
  variables entered/removed in, 133t
regression analysis, 119–121, 130–131, 162
regression coefficients, 121
regression diagnostics, 130–131
regression discontinuity designs, v, 66–67
regression effect, 86
regression equation
  examples of, 122, 134, 135
  formula for, 128
  interaction terms in, 149
  overview of, 117–118, 120–121
  as path analysis, 160
  predictor entry and removal from, 124–125, 136
regression weights (term), 121
relationship effect sizes, 4–5
Relative Fit Index (RFI), 164
relaxation therapy, 50
reliability
  defined, 19, 164
  overview and types of, 8–12
  standard error of measurement relationship to, 29
  as test item function, 35
  validity compared to, 13
reliability coefficients, 13–14, 15, 18
reliability indices, 35, 36, 56

reliability measures, 56
retrospective validity, 18
risk estimates, 46–47
Root Mean Square Error of Approximation (RMSEA), 163
Root Mean Square Residuals (RMR), 163
row main effect, 80

S

SAS computer software
   confidence intervals, calculating with, 49, 51, 53–56, 77
   data, missing, imputation strategies for, 166
   r effect size, calculating with, 38–39
   unbalanced factorial design, approach to, 86
SAS/IML code, 147
SAT scores, 59–61
Scheffe's post hoc procedure, 95
second order interaction, 87
selection in ANCOVA, 101
self-control strategies, 49
self-esteem, 161
semipartial correlation, 124, 128, 129
sequential approach, 86, 88
sequential regression (term), 136
short-term dynamic therapy, 51
simple correlations, limitations of, 129–130
simple linear regression analysis, 119–121, 162
simple regression, assumptions of, 118–119
simple research designs, v
social psychological theory of stereotype threats, 148
social sciences, 35
social sciences research, 35
Somer's D Index of Asymmetrical Association, 114, 116
Spearman Rank-Order correlation (Spearman "rho"), 108–109, 116–117, 117t
specificity, 19
specified value, 34
SPSS computer software
   adjusted R-squared provided by, 131–132, 132t
   analysis of variance, calculating with, 75, 75t, 85–86, 90, 96
   for ANCOVA, 104–107
   for backward elimination, 132, 132t
   balanced and unbalanced designs handled by, 82
   Brown-Forsythe and Welch test results, calculating with, 79
   for coefficients, 120t
   confidence interval, calculating with, 33, 34, 36
   contrasts, running with, 93–94
   correlation linearity assumption, testing with, 116–117
   correlation test size, running with, 68–69
   data, missing, imputation strategies for, 166
   factor analysis using, 16
   for forced method, 134
   Games-Howell post hoc test results, calculating with, 79–80
   for general linear model (GLM) for analysis, 141t
   for group research study, 64
   internal consistency, calculating with, 11–12
   logistic regression withdrawal, running with, 137–138
   for MANOVA, 140, 145–146
   for nested ANOVA design, 97–99
   Process Procedure for, 150–151
   r effect size, calculating with, 38–39
   regression equations in, 149
   scatter plots from, 119
   simple linear regression analysis, 119–121
   for stepwise procedure, 135
   test-retest reliability, calculating with, 10–11
   Tukey procedure, performing with, 96
   for two-predictor case, 124–125
   unbalanced factorial design, approach to, 86–88
squared loadings, 19, 20t
squared multiple correlations, 19
SSA (sum of squares for interaction), 82, 84, 86
SSB (sum of squares between), 4, 82, 84, 126t, 133t, 134t. *See also* UNIQUE sums of squares.
SSB (weighted sum of squares), 73, 74–75
SST (total sum of squares), 4
SSW (sum of squares within), 73–74, 75, 82
standard deviation, 9
standard difference type of effect size, 5
standard error of estimate, 30

standard error of measurement, 28
standard error of validity coefficient, 30
standardized measures, 121
standardized regression coefficients, 121, 161
Standardized Root Mean Square Residual (S-RMR), 163
Stanford Hypnotic Susceptibility Scale, 10–11
state anxiety, 145
statistical software, 165
statistical tests, 36, 40
step down analysis, 25
stepwise procedure, 135
stepwise regression, 124
stereotype-threat hypothesis, 148
structural equations modeling, 136–137, 160–162, 163
structural validity, 18–19
structure coefficients, 17, 130
structure correlations, 17, 130
studentized range statistic, 96
suppressor variables, 127–130
symmetrical correlations, 114, 116

T

test anxiety
    group research design measuring, 63
    hypnotizability versus, 110t
    locus of control effect on, 147
    logistical regression applied to, 136
    nested design studies on, 96–101
    scales (r effect size), 38
    testing for, 66–67, 68–69, 69t, 81–83
Test Anxiety Inventory, 81–83
test-retest reliability, 10–11, 11t, 102
test scores, 9
tetrachoric, 109
textbook validity (term), 15
theory testing, 91
theta as multidimensional reliability coefficient, 13
three-group (defined), 140
three-way ANOVA (analysis of variance), 89–90
three-way interaction, 89
total effect (defined), 161
trait anxiety, 145
transactional analysis, 50
treatment outcome, 45–47, 45t, 51
true experimental research design, 67

true score (term), 8
T squared. *See* Hotelling's T squared
t test.
    for contrast, 92, 94–95
    for independent groups, 63
    modifications of, 95
    normality assumption, robustness to, 126–127
    null hypothesis for, 92
    power for, 157, 165
    squared multivariate generalization of, 26
t-test statistic, 68, 72–73, 75
Tucker-Lewis Fit Index (TLI), 164
Tukey HSD (Honestly Significant Difference), 95–96
Tukey-Kramer procedure, 96
two-group MANOVA (Multivariate Analysis of Variance), 143–147
two group mean comparison, effect size for, 5, 165
two groups, confidence interval for effect size d for, 54–55
two-predictor case, 123–125, 123t, 128–129
two-way ANOVA (analysis of variance), 80, 84, 87–88, 89, 103–104
Type I error (hypothesis testing), 40, 72, 95, 156
Type II error (hypothesis testing), 40, 156

U

unbalanced factorial designs, 86–88
undimensional scales, 8–12
unequal variances, tests for, 77–80
unexplained variation or variance (term), 117
UNIQUE sums of squares, 98t, 99t, 105t, 106t
univariate d, formula for, 26–27, 144
univariate research design, 159
univariate statistics, v, 25–26, 146

V

validity, 13–14, 29–31
validity coefficients
    definition and overview of, 14, 15–16
    obtaining for predictive validity, 16
    reliability coefficients compared to, 13–14, 15, 18
    testing calculated against hypothesized,

28–29
validity indices, 56
variables, correlation between, 127
variances, homogeneity of, 76t, 119
verbal ability, 128

W

weight d, 41–42
Welch and Brown-Forsythe Test for unequal variances, 77–80
Weschler Adults Intelligence Scale (WAIS), 28
Wherry formula, 131
Wilcox-Mann Whitney test, 157
Wilcox signed-rank test, 157
Wilks' Lambda, 140, 165
within group variability, reducing, 158–159
women, underperformance of, 148

X

X*M interaction term, 149

Z

zero, effect size of, 6
Z-scores, 37, 135

CHARLES C THOMAS • PUBLISHER • LTD.

SYSTEMATIC INSTRUCTION OF FUNCTIONAL SKILLS FOR STUDENTS AND ADULTS WITH DISABILITIES
(Second Edition)
by Keith Storey and Craig Miner
2017 • 272 pp. (7 x 10)
14 illustrations • 32 tables
$36.95 (paper) • $26.95 (ebook)

CASE STUDIES IN APPLIED BEHAVIOR ANALYSIS FOR STUDENTS AND ADULTS WITH DISABILITIES
by Keith Storey and Linda Haymes
2016 • 344 pp. (8.5 x 11)
29 illustrations • 4 tables
$53.95 (paper) • $53.95 (ebook)

INTRODUCTION TO HUMAN RELATIONS STUDIES
by George Henderson and Wesley C. Long
2016 • 364 pp. (7 x 10)
$62.95 (paper) • $62.95 (ebook)

THE UNDECIDED COLLEGE STUDENT
(Fourth Edition)
by Virginia N. Gordon and George E. Steele
2015 • 308 pp. (7 x 10)
4 illustrations
$44.95 (paper) • $44.95 (ebook)

CAMPUS CRIME
(Third Edition)
by Bonnie S. Fisher and John J. Sloan, III
2013 • 440 pp. (7 x 10)
13 illustrations • 17 tables
$74.95 (hard) • $54.95 (paper) • $54.95 (ebook)

RESEARCH IN SPECIAL EDUCATION
(Second Edition)
by Phillip D. Rumrill, Jr., Bryan G. Cook and Andrew L. Wiley
2011 • 278 pp. (7 x 10)
2 illustrations • 9 tables
$42.95 (paper) • $42.95 (ebook)

BEING BRIGHT IS NOT ENOUGH
(Third Edition)
by Peggy Hawley
2010 • 174 pp. (7 x 10)
5 illustrations • 2 tables
$32.95 (paper) • $32.95 (ebook)

HELPING STUDENTS WITH DISABILITIES DEVELOP SOCIAL SKILLS, ACADEMIC LANGUAGE AND LITERACY THROUGH LITERATURE STORIES, VIGNETTES, AND OTHER ACTIVITIES
by Elva Durán, Rachael Gonzáles and Hyun-Sook Park
2016 • 608 pp. (8.5 x 11)
$49.95 (comb-paper) • $49.95 (ebook)

RENTZ'S STUDENT AFFAIRS PRACTICE IN HIGHER EDUCATION
(Fifth Edition)
by Naijian Zhang
2016 • 640 pp. (7 x 10)
6 illustrations • 5 tables
$69.95 (hard) • $69.95 (ebook)

LATINO ACCESS TO HIGHER EDUCATION
by Martin Guevara Urbina and Claudia Rodriguez Wright
2015 • 282 pp. (7 x 10)
3 illustrations • 8 tables
$43.95 (paper) • $43.95 (ebook)

ACTIVITIES TO ENHANCE SOCIAL, EMOTIONAL, AND PROBLEM-SOLVING SKILLS
(Third Edition)
by John M. Malouff and Nicola S. Schutte
2014 • 290 pp. (8.5 x 11)
3 illustrations
$46.95 (spiral) • $46.95 (ebook)

DISPROPORTIONALITY IN EDUCATION AND SPECIAL EDUCATION
by Amity L. Noltemeyer and Caven S. McLoughlin
2012 • 288 pp. (7 x 10)
1 illustrations • 5 tables
$41.95 (paper) • $41.95 (ebook)

A SURVIVAL GUIDE FOR NEW FACULTY MEMBERS
by Jeffrey P. Bakken and Cynthia G. Simpson
2011 • 258 pp. (7 x 10)
3 illustrations • 43 tables
$39.95 (paper) • $39.95 (ebook)

VIOLENCE GOES TO COLLEGE
(Second Edition)
by John Nicoletti, Sally Spencer-Thomas and Christopher M. Bollinger
2009 • 392 pp. (7 x 10)
9 illustrations • 8 tables
$64.95 (paper) • $64.95 (ebook)

TO ORDER: 1-800-258-8980 • books@ccthomas.com • www.ccthomas.com